THE APOST

OUTSTANDING CHRISTIAN THINKERS
Series Editor: Brian Davies OP

The series offers a range of authoritative studies on people who have made an outstanding contribution to Christian thought and understanding. The series will range across the full spectrum of Christian thought to include Catholic and Protestant thinkers, to cover East and West, historical and contemporary figures. By and large, each volume will focus on a single 'thinker', but occasionally the subject may be a movement or a school of thought.

Brian Davies OP, the Series Editor, is Vice-Regent of Studies at Blackfriars, Oxford, where he also teaches philosophy. He is a member of the Theology Faculty of the University of Oxford and tutor in theology at St Benet's Hall, Oxford. He has lectured regularly at the University of Bristol, Fordham University, New York, and the Beda College, Rome. He is Reviews Editor of *New Blackfriars*. His previous publications include: *An Introduction to the Philosophy of Religion* (OUP, 1982); *Thinking about God* (Geoffrey Chapman, 1985); and he was editor of *Language, Meaning and God* (Geoffrey Chapman, 1987).

Existing titles in the series:

Anselm
G. R. Evans

Denys the Areopagite
Andrew Louth

Yves Congar
Aidan Nichols OP

Reinhold Niebuhr
Kenneth Durkin

The Apostolic Fathers
Simon Tugwell OP

Planned titles in the series include:

Bede
Benedicta Ward

Aquinas
Brian Davies OP

Karl Rahner
William Dych SJ

John Calvin
John Platt

George Berkeley
David Berman

Teresa of Avila
Rowan Williams

THE APOSTOLIC
FATHERS

Simon Tugwell OP

MOREHOUSE PUBLISHING
HARRISBURG, PENNSYLVANIA

Published in North America by
Morehouse Publishing
Harrisburg, Pennsylvania

Copyright © Simon Tugwell OP 1989

First published in North America 1990

Nihil obstat	Brian Davies OP
	John Farrell OP
Imprimi potest	Timothy Radcliffe OP
	22 November 1988

Library of Congress Cataloging-in-Publication Data
Tugwell, Simon.
    The apostolic Fathers / Simon Tugwell.
      p. cm.—(Outstanding Christian thinkers)
      ISBN 0-8192-1492-2.—ISBN 0-8192-1491-4 (pbk.)
    1. Apostolic Fathers.   2. Theology—Early church, ca.30-600.
    I. Title. II. Series.
    BR67 T84 1990
    270.1—dc20
                                       89-28406
                                          CIP

ISBN 0-8192-1492-2 (hardback)
0-8192-1491-4 (paperback)

Typeset by Colset Private Limited, Singapore
Printed and bound in Great Britain by
Biddles Limited, Guildford and King's Lynn

Contents

Editorial foreword

St Anselm of Canterbury once described himself as someone with faith seeking understanding. In words addressed to God he says 'I long to understand in some degree thy truth, which my heart believes and loves. For I do not seek to understand that I may believe, but I believe in order to understand.'

And this is what Christians have always inevitably said, either explicitly or implicitly. Christianity rests on faith, but it also has content. It teaches and proclaims a distinctive and challenging view of reality. It naturally encourages reflection. It is something to think about; something about which one might even have second thoughts.

But what have the greatest Christian thinkers said? And is it worth saying? Does it engage with modern problems? Does it provide us with a vision to live by? Does it make sense? Can it be preached? Is it believable?

This series originates with questions like these in mind. Written by experts, it aims to provide clear, authoritative and critical accounts of outstanding Christian thinkers from New Testament times to the present. It will range across the full spectrum of Christian thought to include Catholic and Protestant thinkers, thinkers from East and West, thinkers ancient, mediaeval and modern.

The series draws on the best scholarship currently available, so it will interest all with a professional concern for the history of Christian ideas. But contributors will also be writing for general readers who have little or no previous knowledge of the subjects to be dealt with. Volumes to appear should therefore prove helpful at a popular as well as an academic level. For the most part they will be devoted to a single thinker, but occasionally the subject will be a movement or a school of thought.

This book is one of those dealing with more than one thinker. It has become customary to gather under the label of 'The Apostolic Fathers' a motley collection of important and seminal Christian writings dating from between about AD 50 and 150, and it is these to which Simon Tugwell provides an introduction. They give us fascinating glimpses into some of the different ways in which early generations of Christians tried to make sense of their faith and to deal with the problems which had arisen. Fr Tugwell makes us acquainted with a brilliant and passionate martyr (Ignatius of Antioch), a stolid, down-to-earth, primitive canon lawyer (the unknown author of the *Didache*), a spokesman for the church in Rome (Clement of Rome), and others who helped to shape the Christian tradition. As he indicates, their message is often highly pertinent in the new age of anxiety and uncertainty in which Christians live today.

Brian Davies OP

Preface

If we were to organize, with the help of time-machines and science fiction, a symposium at which Christian thinkers from every age were given an opportunity to present their characteristic doctrines, it is likely that the Apostolic Fathers would mostly feel rather out of place. If by 'thinkers' we are going to mean only people who have displayed their intellectual prowess in the deep waters of speculative theology and philosophy, then most of the Apostolic Fathers should not have been invited to our symposium in the first place. But, in a more generous understanding of the word, there is good reason to recognize the Apostolic Fathers as significant Christian thinkers.

The writers whom we now know as 'the Apostolic Fathers' were first rounded up and labelled like this in the late seventeenth century, following a pioneering edition of Barnabas, Hermas, Clement, Ignatius and Polycarp by the French scholar J. B. Cotelier, who dubbed them 'Fathers who flourished in the time of the apostles'. There has in fact been much scholarly controversy as to how many of them, if any, did actually flourish in the time of the apostles, but few scholars would jib at the claim that all the writings assembled under this heading do at any rate fall within the first 120 years of Christian history. That is to say, they belong to the period when the Christian church was struggling to understand its own identity and to define its distinctness from the Judaism which had enfolded its birth. They belong to the period when the church was only gradually beginning to shape its own canon of Scripture, with a 'New Testament' as well as the old Jewish Bible. They belong to the period when the church was progressively formalizing its structures and institutions and, under pressure from various movements and ideologies quickly diagnosed as 'heretical', developing a consciousness of its own 'orthodox' doctrine.

Viewed from the vantage point of posterity, with its superior wisdom, these early writers can easily be seen as rather footling, if not downright weird; but if we try to appreciate their endeavours in their own context, we can recognize that they were engaged in a very serious and very necessary intellectual exercise. In their different ways—and their ways were very different, as were their immediate settings—they were applying their minds to the practical and theoretical issues facing the church. And in a time of widespread confusion, like our own, in which we have seen apparently rocklike structures crumble almost overnight, these strange voices from the past can perhaps speak to us with a new aptness and even familiarity. They were trying to find out, with few points of certainty to guide them, what it meant to be a Christian. The church has maybe, after all, not moved so very far from that primitive and exhilarating problematic.

Indeed, for the generation of the Apostolic Fathers, as for our own, the church herself very often seemed to be the problem. In the eyes of some, who did not want their religion to be too demanding, the church was far too religious; in the eyes of others, who wanted an elaborate ritual life or a chance to sail off splendidly into a spiritual empyrean, the church was not religious enough. It is interesting how much of the writing of the Apostolic Fathers constitutes a kind of apologia for the institutional church.

Since the dating of most of the works discussed is controversial, it would be foolish to claim that they are arranged here in chronological order, though by and large I have followed what I believe to be their chronological sequence. We begin with the *Didache* and Barnabas, two texts whose content makes it appropriate to take them closely together, whether or not they belong together in time. Their essential question is one which must have arisen almost immediately in the early church, and which is close to the Jewish matrix within which Christian speculation inevitably began: What, for a Christian, is the proper understanding of God's law?

Next we turn to two Roman documents, the *Shepherd* of Hermas and the letter of Clement to the Corinthians, both of which, in their different ways, are concerned with what it means to belong to the church. At first sight Hermas looks about as systematic as a rubbish dump, but I hope he will be discovered to have more structural coherence than he has sometimes been credited with. Clement's letter reflects a somewhat more developed ecclesiology than either the *Didache* or Barnabas, and he introduces us to notions which subsequently became routine elements in Catholic theology, such as 'apostolic succession'. After Clement we pass to Ignatius of Antioch, the first writer known to have used the phrase 'the Catholic church', and he is appropriately followed by his friend and admirer, Polycarp of Smyrna. Finally we take up the so-called 'Second Letter of Clement', whose provenance is quite uncertain.

My aim in this book has been to present an interpretation of these various writings, not to give a full account of the innumerable scholarly debates which they provoked. I have tried to take cognizance of the relevant scholarship, but it seemed inappropriate here to append lengthy notes, relating my views to those of other scholars. The primary evidence, from the texts themselves, I have cited as I go along; where it has seemed important or useful, I have provided in the notes some slightly fuller references to ancient sources and to modern dicussions, as well as occasional more detailed arguments of my own. Needless to say, the sparseness of my explicit allusions to their works implies no lack of appreciation of or gratitude to the many scholars whose books and articles have helped me to develop my own understanding of these interesting texts. And I have also benefited enormously over the years from discussions with colleagues and students too numerous to name. I am particularly grateful to Anthony Meredith SJ for reading through the complete typescript with his customary critical acumen.

The editions of the texts that I have used are listed in the bibliography. All translations in this book, including those from Scripture, are my own. For the sake of convenience, I cite biblical books according to the current modern versions, such as the Revised Standard Version. References to the Apostolic Fathers are given in accordance with the standard divisions and subdivisions, which vary hardly at all from edition to edition, except that the useful division of Hermas into continuously numbered paragraphs is not found in editions prior to that included in the series Sources Chrétiennes. I have therefore cited Hermas both by paragraph number and by reference to the older divisions of the text (thus Sim. 5.5, 58.2 = Similitudes 5.5, which, in the new numbering, is paragraph 58, subdivision 2).

Simon Tugwell OP

Bibliography of editions and translations

The most substantial edition of the Apostolic Fathers is that by J. B. Lightfoot, with a large edition of Clement, Ignatius and Polycarp, (5 vols; London, 1885; London, 1890), and a smaller edition of all the Apostolic Fathers, with an English translation, in one volume (London, 1891).

There is an edition, with English translation, by Kirsopp Lake, in the Loeb Classical Library (2 vols, 1912, 1913).

All the Apostolic Fathers, except for Hermas, are included in the 3rd, revised, version of Funk's edition, edited by K. Bihlmeyer (Tübingen, 1970).

There are important editions of all the Apostolic Fathers, except *2 Clement*, in Sources Chrétiennes:

   Didache, ed. W. Rordorf and A. Tuilier (Paris, 1978).
   Barnabas, ed. P. Prigent and R. A. Kraft (Paris, 1971).
   Hermas, ed. R. Joly (Paris, 1968).
   Clement, ed. A. Jaubert (Paris, 1971).
   Ignatius and Polycarp, ed. P. T. Camelot (Paris, 1969).

There is an English translation of the Apostolic Fathers, without Hermas and *2 Clement*, in the Penguin Classics: *Early Christian Writings*, trans. Maxwell Staniforth, with new editorial material by A. Louth (Harmondsworth, Middx, 1987).

Bibliographies will be found in all these editions, but the immense scholarly literature on the Apostolic Fathers is largely made up of very specific, detailed studies. English-speaking readers may, however, like to note:

L. W. Barnard, *Studies in the Apostolic Fathers and their Background* (Oxford, 1966).
Virginia Corwin, *St Ignatius and Christianity in Antioch* (London, 1960).
A. P. O'Hagan, *Material Re-creation in the Apostolic Fathers* (Berlin, 1968).

Abbreviations

Hermas
Mand. Commandments
Sim. Parables (Similitudes)
Vis. Visions

Letters of Ignatius
Eph. Ephesians
Mag. Magnesians
Phld. Philadelphians
Pol. Polycarp
Rom. Romans
Sm. Smyrnaeans
Trall. Tralleans

CD   Qumran, Covenant Document
PG   J.-P. Migne (ed.), *Patrologia Graeca*
PL   J.-P. Migne (ed.), *Patrologia Latina*
1QH Qumran, Hymns of Thanksgiving
1QS Qumran, Rule of the Community

1

The *Didache*

The *Didache* is a rudimentary manual of church order, compiled in the first century AD. Its 'author' has worked into his text at least two earlier documents, which may go back to the very earliest years of Christian history: a brief instruction on Christian morals, which is also known from other sources, and a liturgical directive on baptism and the eucharist. In the adaptation of these documents we can recognize the work of a single editor, who may well be the compiler of the *Didache* as a whole; him we shall call 'the Didachist'. The full title of the book, 'The teaching [Greek *didachē*] of the apostles', indicates the author's intention to pass on what he took to be apostolic tradition.

The church for which the *Didache* was written was clearly a predominantly rural one, and, although the work was certainly known and used in Egypt, it probably originated in some Greek-speaking part of western Syria.

Both the ethical catechesis incorporated into the *Didache* (the 'Two Ways') and the *Didache* itself envisage converts to Christianity from paganism; nevertheless there is an unmistakable Jewish background throughout. The *Didache* belongs in the context of the early Christian attempt to define the new religion as distinct from Judaism.

The picture of the church that we get from the *Didache* is a strange one. We are given an invaluable glimpse of a community that is making or has just made the transition from a régime of prophets and teachers to one of bishops and deacons. The author has to reassure his readers that the liturgy celebrated by these new officials

1

is just as good as that of the prophets and teachers (15.1–2). And it is still regarded as normal and desirable that each local church should have its prophet and teacher. Any authentic prophet or teacher who is willing to stay should be welcomed and supported by the church, 'for they are your high priests' (13.1–3).

One reason why prophets and teachers are so welcome is that this is a church which has not yet developed more than the most basic doctrines about Christian belief and practice. Anyone who can 'add to' its 'righteousness and knowledge of the Lord' is to be received 'as the Lord' (11.2).

This dependence on 'charismatic' leaders, however, posed several problems. First of all, there was the general difficulty, widely encountered in the early Christian centuries, that the hospitality which Christians were expected to practise towards visitors could easily be exploited. This was sufficiently well known for the pagan writer, Lucian, to be able to make a story out of it.[1] The Didachist, therefore, gives some rules to help the community to deal with visitors. 'Everyone who comes in the name of the Lord is to be welcomed', but, after the initial welcome, a more stringent attitude is to be adopted. A traveller is to be helped as much as possible, but he must not stay for more than three days at the outside. If he wants to remain, he must earn his keep by doing some work. The Didachist leaves it to the good sense of the community to decide what to do with someone who has no craft or skills, but in any case no Christian is to be allowed to live in idleness. Any visitor who refuses to abide by these terms is to be shunned as a 'trader in Christ' (12.1–5).

Genuine prophets and teachers, on the other hand, deserve to be supported without having to do any other work. They should be given the first fruits of all the produce and income of the community (13.1–7). But how are genuine teachers to be recognized?

The primary criterion is a doctrinal one. Referring back to the ethical and liturgical instructions which occupy the first ten chapters of the *Didache*, the author says, 'If anyone comes and teaches you all these things, welcome him; but if the teacher turns aside to teach some other doctrine with destructive consequences, do not listen to him' (11.1–2). Any teaching which undermines the 'apostolic tradition', which our compiler has presented to us, is automatically regarded as disqualifying the would-be teacher. New teaching, by contrast, which proposes some development in the understanding of Christian faith and practice, is acceptable, provided it is compatible with what has already been received. In view of the very meagre tradition which is already established—it contains almost no

Christology, for instance—one cannot help but feel that the church of the *Didache* was singularly unprotected against heresy.

Apart from plain teachers, two special kinds of itinerant teacher called for more specific treatment, though they were all naturally still subject to the basic doctrinal criterion.

'Apostles' were expected to conform to a rather stricter version of the rules governing all Christian travellers. They were allowed to stay for only one day, or two if it was necessary; if they stayed for a third day, that was enough to reveal them as 'false prophets'. At their departure they were to be given only enough bread to last them until their next port of call; if they asked for money, once again they were thereby exposed as phoney (11.4–6).

These 'apostles' are evidently not to be identified with the Twelve. They are rather the successors of all the itinerant preachers sent out by Christ (cf. Luke 10:1–11), and they are an important link in the development of the itinerant monasticism characteristic of the Syrian church.[2] The hardening of itinerancy into a rule making it compulsory to move on nearly every day (a rule found later in Manichaean monasticism)[3] was presumably the result of a combination of apostolic urgency and the need to protect the hosts of the wandering preachers from having their hospitality unfairly exploited or overburdened.

Quite what the role of the apostles was is not clear. No liturgical office is ascribed to them; it is only prophets and teachers who are described as celebrating the liturgy (15.1). Nor is there any suggestion that the content of their teaching differed from that of other teachers. The fact of their constant wandering might imply that their task was to provide basic instruction in the faith, which could then be elaborated by more settled teachers. Against this interpretation, however, is the initial rubric which welcomes teachers of any kind who can *add* to the church's 'righteousness and knowledge of the Lord' (11.2), and also the fact that teachers other than apostles are not necessarily going to settle down any more than the apostles do (cf. 13.1–2). It is unlikely that there was any rigorous division of labour between apostles and other teachers, any more than there is now between parochial clergy and visiting preachers. The essential distinction was simply that apostles were not allowed to settle down, whereas other teachers were free to stay or to move on as they pleased or in response to the needs of the churches.

'Prophets' were distinguished from other teachers by the fact that they 'spoke in spirit'. Although it is not clear exactly what 'speaking in spirit' means, it was evidently a phenomenon that could be recognized at once. Presumably the *Didache* is referring to the same phenomenon that St Paul mentions in 1 Cor 12:3, and, like St Paul, it shows an awareness that the 'spirit' in question is not necessarily the Holy Spirit. 'Not everyone who speaks in spirit is a prophet' (11.8). We may presume that, however it was manifested, 'speaking in spirit' involved making utterances purporting to come from God and so claiming the authority of divine revelation. It was therefore crucial to have some criteria whereby to judge whether the alleged revelation was genuine or not, particularly in a church as ill-equipped with doctrine as that of the *Didache*. St Paul proposes a very simple test: if someone speaking in spirit is able to confess that 'Jesus is Lord', the inspiration comes from the Holy Spirit; if instead the person curses Jesus, then it is another spirit that is at work. Since 'speaking in spirit' is evidently not something that goes on entirely beyond the control of the speaker (cf. 1 Cor 14:32), the Pauline test can presumably be applied by requiring the speaker to confess that 'Jesus is Lord' and seeing what happens.

St Paul has no qualms about subjecting both the behaviour and the words of prophets to the critical judgement of the church (1 Cor 14:29–33). The Didachist does not share his confidence. He knows that sins against the Holy Spirit cannot be forgiven and, unlike the New Testament writers, he identifies this kind of sin with presuming to question or discriminate between prophetic utterances (11.7). No doubt a 'prophet' who infringed the rudimentary doctrinal principles governing all sorts of teachers would thereby be disqualified, and the Didachist himself in fact notes other things which someone speaking in spirit might say, which would reveal him to be a false prophet: 'If anyone says in spirit, "Give me money" or anything else, do not listen to him' (11.12). But, for the Didachist, the essential test is how the 'prophet' behaves. What has to be discovered is whether someone who speaks in spirit is or is not a genuine prophet; it is only the words of genuine prophets that cannot be criticized without sinning against the Holy Spirit. Although it may sometimes be possible to convict a false prophet on the basis of what he says, what is looked for primarily is that the prophet should have 'the manners of the Lord' and that he should practise what he preaches. If he asks for money or other gifts, it must be for the benefit of the poor; if he orders a meal 'in spirit', it must be for others, and he must not eat it himself (11.7–12).

A speaker in spirit who passes the test and is recognized as a 'true, tested prophet' (11.10) is exempt from critical assessment. His words must simply be accepted as coming from God. In the church of the *Didache* there can be no question of revelation being already closed and complete. Further revelation was both needed and expected. And if the prophet did strange things, like the prophets of the Old Testament, it was for God to judge him, provided that he did not try to incite his hearers to behave likewise (11.11).

The ethical catechesis adopted and adapted by the Didachist pre-existed the *Didache*, as has already been mentioned. We get a good idea of its contents, before its adaptation by the Didachist, from a Latin version which has survived in two mediaeval manuscripts, known as the *Doctrina Apostolorum*.[4]

The overall structure of this little catechism embodies a teaching device common to Judaism and classical antiquity. The life of virtue and the life of vice are presented as two options or 'ways', with the implication, sometimes explicated, that we should follow the former and shun the latter. In the Jewish tradition, the way of virtue is associated with the promise of life, while the way of vice is associated with the threat of death. The most famous classical example is the story told by Xenophon of the choice of Herakles.[5] In the Old Testament the outstanding instance is Deuteronomy 29 – 30, in which Moses declares the terms of God's covenant with his people and concludes, 'I have set before you life and death, blessing and curse; so choose life' (Deut 30:19).[6]

It is quite likely that, before the Christians took it over, there was already a Jewish 'Two Ways', containing basic ethical instruction for Gentiles who wanted to associate themselves with Judaism. But the basic schema, common to all varieties of Judaism, could be nuanced in different ways to suit the beliefs of the different parties within Judaism, particularly the Pharisees and the Essenes.

The Pharisees (contrary to what is sometimes affirmed) had a real belief in divine grace, but they supposed that God's help is conditional on the individual's choice of the right path. Whatever choice is made by human beings, whether good or bad, is helped by God.[7] Moses' advice to 'choose life' can thus be taken at its face value: the choice is ours.

The Essenes, by contrast, seem to have espoused a much more deterministic view of life.[8] There are even signs that they believed in astrological determinism.[9] For them it is therefore important to determine of what 'spirit' someone is[10]—just as the Christians introduced exorcisms into the pre-baptismal scrutinies to test whether or not the candidate was in the grip of any demon.[11] It is far from clear to what extent the Essenes or the Christians who followed them believed that human beings were free to escape from the domination of whatever spirit, good or bad, was in possession of them.[12]

Against this background, it is probably significant that the Two Ways is found in the *Doctrina Apostolorum* and in the letter of Barnabas in a form which is not reproduced in the *Didache*. Where the *Didache* simply announces that 'there are two ways, one of life and one of death, and there is a great difference between the two ways' (1.1), both the *Doctrina* and Barnabas refer to two angels presiding over the two ways. Barnabas makes the strongest claim: 'On the one way light-bringing angels of God are drawn up, but angels of Satan on the other way. The one is Lord from eternity and to eternity, but the other is the ruler of this present time of lawlessness' (Barn. 18.1–2). Barnabas is explicitly inviting 'anyone who wishes' to follow 'the way of light' (19.1), but the choice of paths is much more fraught than it appears to be in the *Didache*. Barnabas presents us with 'two ways of teaching and power' (18.1). That is to say, the options are not just proposed to our spontaneous choice; each one is urged upon us, not only with the recommendation of its own appropriate teacher, but with all the power that is at the disposal of that teacher, whether it be God or Satan. At least to some extent, therefore, the exposition of the two ways is almost a diagnostic tool, to alert us to the identity of the power to which we are subject.

The *Didache* has a less sombre view of this present age. It nowhere alludes to any pressure brought to bear on us by hostile spiritual powers. Even in the grim conditions of the Last Days, the opposition comes only from false prophets and 'corrupters' and from a general increase in lawlessness, culminating in the appearance of the 'world-deceiver' (16.3–4). And the false prophets seem to be motivated by common human greed rather than by diabolical inspiration. It is in line with this relatively unthreatening scenario that the Didachist seems to be able to dispense with the idea of our being dramatically rescued by God from the tyranny of Satan; 'redemption', for him, simply means the provision that is made almost routinely for the forgiveness of our sins. If we choose to follow the right path, there is seemingly nothing to hinder us except our own weakness and mistakes.

In spite of some divergences between them, the *Didache* and the *Doctrina* both offer essentially the same account of the ways of life and death, and, particularly in the *Doctrina*, there is a perceptible, if loose, underlying structure. As presented in the *Doctrina*, the way of life begins with a conventional summary of the Law:

> First, you shall love the God who made you; secondly you shall love your neighbour as yourself, and do not do to anyone else anything you want not to be done to you. (1.2)

What follows is said to be the 'interpretation' of this summary.[13] It contains, first, a list of precepts, which is clearly meant to cover the essentials of the Ten Commandments,[14] and then some moral advice which is meant to reinforce these precepts. Then there is a section which explains in more detail how relationships within the community ought to work, which is presumably the 'interpretation' of the second part of the initial summary of the Law.

The list of precepts, although perhaps based on the Ten Commandments, expands them to provide a more thorough outline of the moral standards which Jews and Christians alike wanted to assert over against what were taken to be the typical vices of the Gentiles. Thus the commandment not to commit adultery is enlarged to include a ban on pederasty and fornication, and there is a comprehensive prohibition of magic, whether worked by spells or by potions. Abortion and the killing of new-born babies are both forbidden. The commandment not to bear false witness is expanded into a fairly elaborate list of ways in which we are not to do down our neighbour, culminating, in the *Doctrina*, with the commandment, 'You shall hate no one, and some people you shall love more than your own life' (2.7).

At first sight, it is only the 'social' commandments which are taken up in the precepts of the Two Ways, not those concerning our relationship with God. But this is probably a misleading impression. It is true that all the precepts appear to have a primary reference to how human beings behave towards one another, but it is not true to say, without further ado, that 'the whole of the first part of the decalogue is omitted'.[15] The first two commandments, if taken together,[16] amount to a ban on idolatry, and the second section of the Two Ways makes it clear that one of the objectionable things about magic and related interests is that they lead to idolatry (Did. 3.4).[17] The commandment not to take the Lord's name in vain is represented in the precepts by the ban on perjury (2.3),[18] and it can probably be recognized in the second section in the comments on the sort of things that lead to blasphemy (3.6).[19]

What is undoubtedly missing from the Two Ways is the commandment to keep the Sabbath[20] and the commandment to honour

7

father and mother. The omission of the former can be explained simply by the fact that Christians did not celebrate the Sabbath and evidently the compiler of the Two Ways saw no reason to pretend that they did, albeit in a new sense.[21] The omission of the commandment to honour father and mother presumably reflects the situation which the gospels underline in stark and exaggerated terms (cf. Luke 14:26): the followers of Jesus must choose him at whatever cost to their family loyalties. Rather than honouring father and mother, they are to honour anyone who speaks the word of God to them (Did. 4.1). The cohesion of the family is superseded by the cohesion of the Christian community (4.2–3). It was only later on, when the Church was more securely established in society, that Christians could stop being embarrassed by the fifth commandment.[22]

The Didachist takes over the list of precepts almost unchanged, but he has considerably altered its significance: instead of presenting it as the interpretation of the initial summary of the Law, he supplies a new interpretation of the summary and relegates the list of precepts to being 'the second commandment' (2.1).

The new 'interpretation' bears a pronounced likeness to certain parts of the Sermon on the Mount, though it is sufficiently different to show that the author is drawing on the same tradition as St Matthew, rather than on Matthew himself. Loving our neighbour, it turns out, means responding with good will and even love to those who hate and persecute us. It means being sufficiently free from 'fleshly and bodily desires' to be able to turn the other cheek, when someone strikes us, and to go a second mile with someone who forces us to go one mile, and to give our cloak to someone who appropriates our coat. With a wry humour that perhaps deliberately lowers the ideological tone, the author goes on, 'If anyone takes what belongs to you away from you, do not claim it back, because you cannot anyway' (1.5).

The last item in this section of the Two Ways in the *Didache* gives us an interesting glimpse of how Christian thought developed. It begins with the general commandment (found also in Matt 5:42), 'Give to everyone who asks and do not claim anything back'. A precept like this obviously laid Christians wide open to being mercilessly exploited by unscrupulous scroungers. Two lines of defence are adopted in the *Didache*, both of them perhaps already traditional, though it is likely that the unmitigated doctrine presented in the Sermon on the Mount is a truer account of what Christ himself taught. First of all, an attempt is made to discourage scroungers:

Blessed is anyone who gives in accordance with the commandments, for he is blameless. But woe to the recipient! Anyone who receives something when he needs it will be blameless, but if he does not need it, he will be called to account for why he accepted it and what his purpose was. He will be held in prison and examined about his deeds and he will not come out of there until he has paid the last farthing. (1.5–6)

The second line of defence is provided by a 'saying' which probably derives from Ecclesiasticus 12:1: 'Let your alms sweat in your hands until you know to whom you are to give them' (1.6). There can be little doubt that this dictum is intended to allow for much more selectiveness in almsgiving than would be permitted under a straightforward application of the rule, 'Give to everyone who asks'.

That the commentary tones down the rule is clear. On the face of it, the church is engaging in just that substitution of human tradition for divine law which Christ condemns in Matt 15:3–9. But Christ himself uses a similar exegetical technique (derived from the Pharisees) to justify his own and his disciples' failure to observe the Sabbath (cf. Luke 6:1–4; 13:15–16). And in some cases it is difficult to see how the commandments could be observed at all, unless they are tempered in this way by realism. At any rate, this tempering of precept by realism is a procedure which is characteristic of the Didachist, as we shall see.

The list of specific precepts which the Didachist inherited from the traditional Two Ways has, as we noted, become in the *Didache* the 'second commandment'. Whether the Didachist was conscious of the implications of this, it is hard to say. After his insertion of his own new interpretation of the summary of the Law, he needed some editorial device to introduce the precepts, and maybe there is no more to be said about it than that. However, if we take his text at its face value, the precepts no longer count as the detailed exposition of what it means to love our God and our neighbour and they therefore no longer have any overt connection with the general principles which were presented as summing up the whole of the Way of Life. It is tempting to accept the suggestion made by some scholars that the 'second commandment' is to be seen as inferior,[23] in which case the Didachist must be working on the principle that 'love covers a multitude of sins' (Prov 10:12; 1 Pet 4:8). That love, in the form of generosity, constitutes an antidote to our sins was a commonplace in Jewish and Christian tradition, and it is mentioned in the *Didache* and the *Doctrina* (4.5–7). And it would not be out of keeping with what the Didachist says elsewhere if he did deliberately accept the inference that fidelity to the details of morality matters less than fidelity to the evangelical picture of Christian charity.

At the end of the list of precepts there is a development which can probably be attributed to the Didachist. Where the *Doctrina* simply bids us hate no one and love some people more than our own lives, the *Didache* has a more elaborate precept:

> You shall not hate anyone, but some people you shall rebuke, for some you shall pray, and some you shall love more than your life. (2.7)

This can be seen as another instance of 'Pharisaic' development and particularization of the Law.

The precepts are followed by more general advice of a sapiential kind. In both the *Doctrina* and the *Didache* one salient feature of this section is that much of it is formulated in terms of encouragement not 'to become' a bad-tempered, envious, quarrelsome person and so on, rather than in simple prohibitions, such as we found in the list of precepts ('you shall not murder' etc.). The catechist's concern here is at least akin to the famous rabbinic policy of 'setting a fence around the Law':[24] to prevent people from breaking the commandments, principles are devised which will keep them at a safe distance from any infringement of the Law. Thus the commandment not to murder is protected by the instruction not to become bad-tempered or envious or quarrelsome or choleric, because all these things lead to murder (3.2). Similarly a lustful person, given to 'dirty talk' and a roving eye, is likely to end up committing adultery or fornication (3.3).

The Two Ways' fence around the Law is patently similar to that erected in the Sermon on the Mount, but it is rather less rigorous. Where Christ attaches an equal moral significance to being angry with your brother and to killing him, to looking lustfully at a woman and to committing adultery with her (Matt 5:22, 27–28), so that loss of temper or a lustful look become sins in their own right, incurring the same penalty as murder or adultery, the Two Ways objects to quarrelsomeness and lustfulness because they lead to real sin; and it accordingly focuses its attention, not on specific acts of bad temper or lust, but on the risk of acquiring settled traits of character which will make someone prone to sins like murder or fornication.

Although the sequence is slightly wrong in both the *Doctrina* and the *Didache*, it looks as if the sapiential section is intended to go with the precepts fairly closely, so that the two sections may be allowed to interpret each other. Thus, although the ban on magic in the precepts is not explicitly related to the biblical commandment not to worship alien gods, the corresponding passage in the sapiential section gives a more general warning against any participation in or even curiosity about pagan superstitions, on the grounds that they lead to idolatry.

Rather interestingly, the ban on thieving[25] is backed initially by the advice not to become a liar, which suggests a different objection to lying from the one contained in the precepts, where 'false, empty speech' is condemned in the context of bearing false witness against people (2.5). Less surprisingly, theft is also said to be the consequence of being greedy for money and being fond of vain glory (3.5).

The structure of what follows has been misconstrued by recent commentators, who have wanted to find in the Two Ways an account of 'the ideal of poverty',[26] which seems to be quite foreign to the *Didache*. 3.6–10 belong together as an expansion of the curt commandment in 2.3 not to commit perjury (which is one of the most serious ways of taking the Lord's name in vain). The protection offered to this commandment consists of advice about how to avoid blasphemy (speaking ill of God). 'My child, do not become a grumbler ... or stubborn or mean-minded'; instead, we are exhorted to become 'meek, because the meek will inherit the earth', and to become patient and merciful and free from malice, to become quiet and good and to tremble at the words of God (cf. Isaiah 66:2). We should not be too keen to push ourselves forward or be too self-assertive, nor should we identify ourselves with people who are like that; we should consort with righteous and humble people. Finally, 'You shall accept as good the things that happen to you, knowing that nothing occurs without God' (3.6–10).[27]

The expansion of the precepts governing social relationships gives us a vignette of the domestic life of the community. Everything is focused on the word of God, unfolded in the words of the 'saints' (faithful Christians). 'My child, you shall remember by night and by day the person who speaks the word of God to you, and you shall honour him as the Lord.' The speaking of God's word has an almost sacramental value, since the Lord is present where his Lordship is being talked about. 'Every day you shall seek out the presence of the saints, so that you can rest in their words' (4.1–2). Later on in the *Didache* we learn that the eucharist is to be celebrated

11

every Sunday (14.1), but the staple diet of the community is its daily exploration of God's word. In the apocalyptic last section of his compilation, the Didachist underlines this with a special urgency:

> Come together frequently to seek what is useful to your souls, because the whole time of your faith will not help you, if you are not made perfect at the last time. In the last days false prophets will multiply . . . (16.2–3)

The unity and fidelity of the community must be maintained by all its members. 'You shall not create any schism, but make peace between people who are fighting. You shall judge justly, and rebuke faults without regard for the position of the offender.' Rather cryptically the text goes on, 'You shall not be in two minds whether it will be or not', which probably means that there is to be no doubt about God's judgement of everyone, however distinguished they may be.

Generosity between the brethren is to be such that people do not consider anything to be their own. Christians, who share together in what is immortal, ought all the more to share their mortal goods with one another:

> Do not become the kind of person who stretches out his hands to receive, but pulls them back when it comes to giving. If you have anything through the work of your hands, you can give it away as a ransom for your sins. Do not hesitate to give and do not grumble when you have made a gift.

Children are to be brought up severely in the fear of God, and Christian slaves are not to be ordered about harshly, lest they lose their fear of the God who rules over slaves and masters alike. When God comes, he will not respect people's social position. All the same, slaves are to be subject to their masters as embodying a manifestation (a 'type') of God (4.1–11).

The Way of Life ends with a general warning to hate anything that is not pleasing to God and not to abandon the Lord's commandments, but to keep them, just as they have been transmitted, neither adding anything nor subtracting anything from them. The *Doctrina* concludes with the instruction, 'Do not go to prayer with a bad conscience', which the *Didache* fills out, so that it reads, 'You shall confess your sins in the church and not go to your prayer with a bad conscience' (4.12–14).

The Didachist clearly takes it for granted that at least some Christians continue to be sinners. The Sunday Mass begins with a confes-

12

sion of sins (14.1), and the eucharistic prayer concludes with the invitation, 'If anyone is holy, let him come; if anyone is not holy, let him repent. Maranatha' (10.6). This is much more benign than the corresponding text in the Apocalypse (Rev 22:10–2), 'The time is near. Let the unrighteous be unrighteous still, let the defiled be defiled still, and let the righteous still work righteousness and the saint still be sanctified. Behold, I am coming quickly . . .'

In the *Didache* there does not seem to be any question of a radical division between saints and sinners. People should aspire to be saints, but, if they sin, they can always repent and undertake works of generosity as a 'ransom' from their sins. This undramatic attitude is another indication of a Pharisaic background to the *Didache*.[28]

The Way of Death is simply a list of variegated nastinesses which, if persisted in, will lead to death (damnation). The *Doctrina* soberly bids the reader abstain from all of them. The *Didache*, perhaps more kindly, ends with the prayer, 'May you be rescued from all these things, my children' (5.2).

The *Doctrina* and the *Didache* conclude with a warning against being led astray from the teaching of the Two Ways (6.1). The Didachist, however, true to his realism and optimism, adds a rider:

> If you can carry the whole yoke of the Lord, you will be
> perfect; but if you cannot, do what you can. (6.2)

Various subtle interpretations have been placed on these words, but they are probably better taken at their face value. There is no reason to suppose that the Didachist means that there are certain commandments which are compulsory, beyond which there are optional (probably ascetic) counsels, which belong to perfection. Nor does it seem plausible to imagine that the Didachist is connecting perfection with complete observance of the Jewish Law, while refusing to make such observance compulsory. Least of all can the interpretation be sustained which would connect perfection with the 'evangelical' section added by the Didachist in 1.3–6, while everyone is bound at least to love God and neighbour.[29] The 'evangelical' section is presented as being the interpretation of what it means to love God and neighbour, so cannot be taken as indicating a perfection beyond these two basic virtues.[30] The Didachist is surely presuming on the optimistic principle of the Pharisees, that keeping even one of the commandments is tantamount to keeping them all,[31] in as much as it shows a basic intention to remain faithful to God's covenant. Granted this fundamental fidelity, any sins that people may commit can always be forgiven.[32]

It is only in connection with diet that the Didachist is interested in laying down a minimum requirement:

> With regard to food, bear what you can, but be very wary of anything sacrificed to idols, because that is worshipping dead gods. (6.3)

Presumably the author is encouraging people to go as far as they can in observing the full Jewish dietary laws,[33] but the essential thing is that they must at least abstain totally from anything offered to idols.

The Didachist's position falls between the much more daring attitude of St Paul and the rather more timid position adopted at the 'Jerusalem Council'. According to Acts 15:29, the assembled apostles decided that the necessary minimum to be imposed on all believers was that they should abstain from 'things sacrificed to idols, from blood and from animals that have been strangled', which subjects the Gentiles compulsorily to more of the Jewish dietary law than the Didachist does. St Paul, on the other hand, believes that Christians can, in principle, eat anything they like, including meat offered to idols (since idols are no real gods anyway). But because some people might be scandalized by seeing their fellow Christians eating certain things (not least meat offered to idols), St Paul calls for self-restraint out of deference to the weaker brethren (Rom 14:1–23, 1 Cor 8:1–13).

The Didachist's little rule seems eminently sensible and realistic. He does not expect ordinary Christians to make complicated judgements about whether or not any item on the menu is likely to cause scandal, as St Paul does. Nor does he lay any great burden on anyone. He does not oblige anyone either to keep or to stop keeping the Jewish dietary laws, nor does he attempt to impose part of the Jewish discipline on anyone. He contents himself with a clear, practical rule which will suffice to keep Christians at a safe distance from pagan worship.

The liturgical section of the *Didache* shows typical signs both of the background we have learned to recognize and of the editorial work of the Didachist. Evidently the inherited tradition concerning the administration of baptism specified that both the celebrant and the candidate should fast before the sacrament is celebrated, a rule which is attested elsewhere in Jewish Christian circles (7.4).[34] Similarly Jewish Christian is the requirement that baptism should be administered in 'living water' (7.1), no doubt a survival into Christianity of the Jewish regulations about what kind of water could be used in purification rites.[35] But the Didachist, realist that he is, adapts the rule almost out of existence:

> If you do not have living water, baptize in some other water. If you cannot baptize in cold water, use warm water. If you have not got either, then pour water three times on the candidate's head in the name of the Father and of the Son and of the Holy Spirit. (7.2–3)

Before baptism the candidate is to be instructed in the ethical catechesis we have just been looking at (7.1).

Fasting and set times of prayer seem to have posed a problem in the Didachist's church. It looks as if some people were imitating Jewish practices.[36] The Didachist, always ready to give precise rules when they are needed, has a simple solution. The Jews (and therefore the Judaizers too) fast on Mondays and Thursdays. The Christians should accordingly not fast on these days, but on Wednesdays and Fridays (8.1). And, instead of reciting Jewish prayers, the Christians should say the Lord's Prayer three times a day (8.2–3).

The eucharistic prayers prescribed by the Didachist raise all kinds of questions about liturgical history.[37] They are based on Jewish prayers of blessing, but they are given a specific Christian content. The only Christological title used is 'Jesus your Servant', and he is seen chiefly as the imparter of knowledge to the church. He has revealed the identity of the 'holy vine of David' (the church, that is), and he has revealed 'life and knowledge' (9.2–3) or 'knowledge and faith and immortality' (10.2). But he is also the one through whom we are given, not just the everyday food and drink which everyone enjoys, but spiritual food and drink and eternal life (10.3).

The structure of both the two prayers is the same: thanksgiving followed by petition. And the petition in each case is eschatological: 'As this broken bread, scattered on the mountains and brought together, became one, so may your church be gathered from the ends of the earth into your kingdom' (9.4). 'Remember your church, Lord, to deliver her from all evil and make her perfect in your love, and gather her from the four winds, sanctified, into your kingdom which you have prepared for her. Let grace come and let this world pass' (10.5–6).

There is, surprisingly, no reference to the Last Supper and no reference to the death and resurrection of Jesus. Apart from the gift of revelation and knowledge, nothing is said to suggest that the coming of Christ has made any essential difference to our situation. Grace is looked forward to at the end of the world, rather than celebrated as a present reality, and the community's hope is definitely focused on the gathering in and perfecting of the church at the end, rather than on any redemption which is now available. On the other hand, the 'spiritual food and drink' alluded to must refer to the eucharist itself, and its association with eternal life implies that it is the food which nurtures those who receive it for eternal life. And it is quite possible that there is a eucharistic significance in the thanksgiving which opens the second prayer: 'We thank you, holy Father, for your holy Name, which you have made to tabernacle in our hearts'.[38] At the very least, this prayer attests the belief that the church, and probably the individual Christian, is the new Temple in which God's Name dwells, and it is possible that God's 'Name' is meant to refer to Christ himself.[39]

Even on the most generous interpretation, however, there seems to be very little awareness of what God has done for us in Christ.

The concluding section of the *Didache*, which is incomplete in the only known manuscript, concerns the Last Days. After the final trials and tribulations and the manifestation of the 'world-deceiver', 'the signs of truth will appear': first, the 'sign of stretching out' will appear in heaven (probably the sign of the cross), then the sound of a trumpet, and thirdly the resurrection of the dead. Then 'the world will see the Lord coming above the clouds of heaven' (16.1–8). At this point the manuscript breaks off, but the paraphrase in a later compilation allows us to infer that the judgement came next.[40]

There are two elements in this little apocalypse which call for comment. First, the mention of the resurrection is qualified by the rider, 'Not the resurrection of everyone, but, as it says, "The Lord will come and all his holy ones with him"' (16.7). This is probably to be taken, not as meaning that dead sinners never get resurrected, but as referring to a preliminary resurrection of the saints before the millennial earthly reign of Christ, which was widely believed in the early church to come before the final judgement, for which all the dead will be raised.

Secondly, the warning that 'the whole time of your faith will not avail you, if you are not made perfect in the last time' (16.2) is, at first sight, difficult to square with the Didachist's relaxed attitude to perfection in 6.2. From 1.4 and 6.2 we learn that, in the Didachist's view, perfection is possible in this life, but it is still worth doing what we can, even if we are unable to achieve perfection. In the eucharist the church prays to be made perfect (10.5) in a context which certainly allows us to regard the perfection of the church as something hoped for at the end. If the perfection of the church includes the perfection of all her members, we can interpret 16.2 as meaning, quite strictly, that faith is useless unless it results in the believer being made perfect precisely at the end (presumably by that gift of God which is asked for in the eucharistic prayer). There is nothing in the context of 16 to suggest that the author is retracting his own earlier words. What is crucial in the last days is faith: 'Those who remain in their faith will be saved' (16.5). The message is the same as in the letter of Barnabas: 'The whole time of our life and faith will avail nothing if we do not now, in the lawless time, and in the coming hazards, resist as befits children of God' (Barn. 4.9). If we take 'faith' (as we probably should) as meaning primarily fidelity, the Didachist's message can be read quite coherently as meaning that all those who remain faithful, who do not abandon the church in the testing times of the last days, will be saved and made perfect, when God brings his church to perfection and gathers it in from the four winds. Even an imperfect obedience to the commandments can be sufficient to demonstrate the fidelity of one's purpose, but there is no room for imperfection in the hereafter. The final test, therefore, will be whether one's loyalty to Christ and his church is paramount, in spite of continuing moral imperfection, or whether one's moral imperfection creates a weakness in faith which will cause one to apostatize under the pressures of the last days. In the latter case, the fact that one was a believer for years will not suffice to outweigh one's eventual apostasy.

Although there is little speculative theology in the *Didache*, this short manual gives us an interesting and quite attractive picture of a rather under-developed Christian community trying to make sense of itself and to deal with the problems it faced. The predominant influence seems to come from converts from Pharisaism, and their religion is in some ways little more than a reformed and simplified Pharisaism. The Didachist appreciated the value of clear legal definitions, even if he was not sensitive to the dangers which St Paul saw in the Pharisees' understanding of perfection. If his religion was perhaps somewhat bland, by comparison with the much more dramatic vision of the difference wrought by Christ which we find in a great deal of the New Testament, it is only fair to remark that something of his common sense and realism had to prevail, sooner or later, in the church. It is strangely reassuring to find that, even in the first century, there were Christians who were fully conscious of being Christians, not Jews, yet who were apparently untouched by the sensationalism attendant upon the novelty of Christianity and the liberation it brought people.

Notes

1 Lucian (mid-second century), in his 'exposure' of the philosopher Peregrinus, presents him as, for a time, exploiting Christian generosity (*De Morte Peregrini* 11-13, 16). When he was obliged to leave home, he wandered around, 'having the Christians as sufficient provisions for his journey' (16). Whether Lucian's picture of Peregrinus is in any way true or fair, it is hard to judge. Aulus Gellius certainly speaks of him in much more respectful terms (*Noctes Atticae* 12.11).

2 Cf. Robert Murray, 'The features of the earliest Christian asceticism' in Peter Brooks (ed.), *Christian Spirituality* (London, 1975), pp. 63-77.

3 Cf. A. Vööbus, *History of Asceticism in the Syrian Orient* I (Louvain, 1958), p. 117 note 34; E. de Stoop, *Vie d'Alexandre l'Acémète* (Patrologia Orientalis VI; Turnhout, 1971), p. 656 note 10.

4 The relationships between the main known examples of the Two Ways have been definitively clarified by J. P. Audet, *La Didachè* (Paris, 1958), pp. 121-63, whose conclusion that the Latin *Doctrina* gives us the most primitive form, and that the *Didache* and Barnabas represent independent adaptations of the original schema, has been generally accepted by scholars. But it is going too far to claim (as is done by J. Liébaert, for instance: *Les Enseignements Moraux des Pères Apostoliques* [Gembloux, 1970], p. 101) that the *Doctrina* represents a 'purely Jewish' tradition.

5 Xenophon, *Mem.* II 1.21-34 (taken from Prodicus).

6 In post-biblical Jewish literature, there is a good example in the Testaments of the Twelve Patriarchs (Asher 12).

7 Cf. Josephus, *Bell. Jud.* II, 8.14, and texts cited in A. Cohen, *Everyman's Talmud* (London, 1949), p. 94, and G. F. Moore, *Judaism* I (Cambridge, Mass., 1927), p. 456; cf. also E. P. Sanders, *Paul and Palestinian Judaism* (London, 1977), p. 224.

8 Cf. Josephus, *Ant. Jud.* XIII, 5.9. If we assume, as is usually and probably rightly done, that the sectarians of Qumran, known to us from the Dead Sea Scrolls, were Essenes, this is borne out by G. Vermes, *The Dead Sea Scrolls in English* (Harmondsworth, Middx, 1975), pp. 75-8.

9 Cf. Vermes, *op. cit.*, pp. 268-70.

10 Ibid., p. 80.

11 Hippolytus, *Apostolic Tradition* 20; *Testamentum Domini* II, 6-7.

12 Cf. E. H. Merrill, *Qumran and Predestination* (Leiden, 1975).

13 Both the twofold commandment of love and the 'Golden Rule' are known from Jewish sources as ways of summarizing the essentials of the Law: cf. Philo, *Spec. Leg.* 2.63; Test. Daniel 5.3; Babylonian Talmud, *Shab.* 31a (cf. Sanders, *op. cit.*, p. 113). In this last text, Hillel describes all the rest of the Law as 'interpretation' of the Golden Rule.

14 Cf. G. Bourgeault, *Décalogue et Morale Chrétienne* (Paris/ Montreal, 1971), pp. 27–74.

15 Liébaert, *op. cit.*, p. 106.

16 As they apparently are, slightly later, in Theophilus of Antioch, *Ad Autolycum* 3.9, ed. R. M. Grant (Oxford, 1970), pp. 112–13, with Grant's note.

17 The Latin text of the *Doctrina* says 'superstition', where the *Didache* has 'idolatry', but this may be due to the adaptation of the Latin to a later situation in which idolatry was not such a real threat.

18 Philo (*Decal*. 82–95) interprets the third commandment almost exclusively with reference to swearing, seeing perjury as the chief way of breaking it.

19 The commandment not to take the Lord's name in vain was the only one about which there was any doubt as to whether sins against it could be forgiven (cf. Sanders, *op. cit.*, pp. 159–60); it is probably this doubt which explains why Hermas thought that 'blasphemy' was the crucial factor in deciding whether or not sinners could be forgiven (Sim. 9.19, 96.3).

20 Also omitted by Theophilus, *loc. cit.*

21 As is done by Justin, for instance (*Dial*. 12.3).

22 It is included by Theophilus, for instance (*loc. cit.*).

23 Cf. E. Peterson, *Frühkirche, Judentum und Gnosis* (Rome/Freiburg/ Vienna, 1959), p. 149; W. Rordorf and A. Tuilier in their Sources Chrétiennes edition of the *Didache* (Paris, 1978), p. 148.

24 Aboth 1.1.

25 The omission of this precept from the *Doctrina* is probably accidental.

26 Audet, *op. cit.*, pp. 308–20; Liébaert, *op. cit.*, p. 108; Rordorf and Tuilier, *op. cit.*, p. 155.

27 The link between this final point and the avoidance of blasphemy is clear from the saying of Akiba quoted in Sanders, *op. cit.*, p. 169: it is pagans who curse their gods when things go badly, an example which is not to be followed.

28 Cf. Sanders, *op. cit.*, p. 203.

29 The first two views are mentioned by Liébaert, who favours the second of them (*op. cit.*, p. 115). The third is proposed by Rordorf and Tuilier, *op. cit.*, pp. 32–4. There is absolutely nothing in the *Didache* to suggest any distinction between precepts and counsels, and it is unlikely that the Didachist, who is so opposed to Judaizing observances in 8, should here be recommending the adoption of the whole Jewish Law; as Rordorf and Tuilier comment, the 'whole yoke of the Lord' must refer to the Law of Christ, not the Law of Moses.

30 Cf. the non-canonical version of the story of the Rich Young Man, in which Christ denies his claim to have been keeping all the commandments, since he has not used his wealth to help the poor (cf. J. Jeremias, *Unknown Sayings of Jesus* [London, 1964], pp. 44–7).

31 Cf. Sanders, *op. cit.*, p. 131, and the whole section pp. 128–47.

32 The belief that it is worth doing what you can, even if it is not very much, reappears later on in the Syriac *Liber Graduum* 24.3–8.

33 This is the prevailing theory, but it is possible that the Didachist is referring only to some set of Jewish 'Laws for Gentiles', of which the

decree of the 'Jerusalem council' is really an instance (cf. H. Maccoby, *Early Rabbinic Writings* [Cambridge, 1988], pp. 144–7).

34 Cf. Clementine Homilies 13.9.3; Clementine Recognitions 7.34; Justin, *I Apol.* 61.2.

35 Cf. Clementine *Diamartyria* 1.2; Clementine Recognitions 4.32. On the importance of 'living water' in Jewish purification rites, cf., in the Mishnah, *Mikwaoth* 1.8, and the debate between the schools of Hillel and Shammai (cf. S. Giet, *L'Enigme de la Didaché* [Paris, 1970], p. 194 note 23).

36 In spite of Audet's ingenious attempt to show otherwise, it seems best to take 'hypocrite' in *Did.* 8 as referring to Judaizers (cf. Gal 2:13). It is Jews who fasted on Monday and Thursday (cf. Moore, *op. cit.*, II, p. 260).

37 Cf. A. Vööbus, *Liturgical Traditions in the Didache* (Stockholm, 1968).

38 There is a textual uncertainty here: one version has 'in our hearts', one has 'in us', both of which could in fact be alternative translations of the same Hebrew or Aramaic original. The former reading would imply divine indwelling in the individual, the latter would at least be open to the interpretation 'in us', i.e. in the church as a whole.

39 On 'Name' as a Christological title, see J. Daniélou, *The Theology of Jewish Christianity* (London, 1964), pp. 147–63.

40 Apostolic Constitutions VII, 32.

2

The Letter of Barnabas

Little can be said with certainty about the author of the Letter of Barnabas except that he liked blackberries (7.8). But it seems tolerably safe to conjecture, on the basis of what he says, that he was an itinerant teacher (cf. 1.4–5), such as we have encountered in the *Didache*, even though he disclaims any such title for himself (1.8, 4.9). Indeed, he gives us a valuable glimpse of such a teacher at work. The Christian 'teacher', judging from New Testament usage (cf. Matt 23:8), was the equivalent of the Jewish rabbi; as such, it was his task to pore over the essential documents of his religion and pass on to his hearers or readers whatever he thought they would benefit from (cf. 1.5). A major part of this task was naturally the study and exegesis of Scripture—and for Barnabas this still means the Old Testament; one apparent reference to a New Testament text as 'scripture' (4.14) is best seen as a mistaken identification as 'scripture' of a bit of Christian tradition. For a rabbi of the first or second century, whether Christian or Jewish, exegesis meant something very different from what it means to a modern scholar, and involved kinds of ingenuity which a twentieth-century reader is likely to find disconcerting. One little nugget of interpretation with which Barnabas was evidently delighted, and of which he even seems rather proud, proves that Abraham's circumcision of 318 members of his household shows that he was really looking ahead to Christ: in the Greek system of using letters of the alphabet as numerals, 18 yields IE (which obviously stands for IESUS) and 300 yields T (which naturally signifies the cross). 'God knows', Barnabas writes, 'No one has ever learned a more noble word from me; but I know that you are worthy of it' (9.7–9). It is worth noting that this particular gem only works in Greek, as the Hebrew numerals would suggest neither Jesus nor the cross.

How much of Barnabas's exegesis is original it is impossible to say; he was certainly drawing on one or more Christian traditions of interpretation, but it is with something of the air of a conjuror producing a rabbit from a hat that he keeps on showing how the most unpromising bits of the Bible, treated with sufficiently devious cleverness, can be persuaded to mean something to do with Christ or his church. There is an aura of personal triumph in his exclamation, 'Once again you have here too the glory of Jesus; it is all in him and pointing to him' (12.7).

If Barnabas refuses the title of 'teacher', this is probably more than conventional literary modesty. His disclaimers reveal an awareness of the role of a teacher in the church of him who forbade his followers to be called 'rabbi' on the grounds that they are all brethren under one teacher (Matt 23:8). As the *Didache* makes clear, it is the responsibility of all believers to come together regularly to seek out 'what is fitting for your souls' (*Did.* 16.2), an injunction which Barnabas repeats (4.10). Within this common enterprise of research into God's will, a teacher who can contribute to the community's growth in understanding and righteousness is to be welcomed, but not uncritically (*Did.* 11.1–2). As a traveller and as a student, the teacher may be expected to possess a broader and deeper appreciation of God's revelation, as it is received through the tradition of the church, but Barnabas can be taken seriously when he says, 'I will show you a few things, not as a teacher, but as one of you' (1.8). The community may choose to recognize someone as a 'teacher', but it is not a role anyone can claim for himself. The essential relationship between the teacher and his flock is conditioned by the fact that they are all fellow disciples of Christ.

Nevertheless, even if he refuses the title, Barnabas's perspective is that of a minister of the word. Like the apostle Paul, he sees his own salvation and his own eternal reward as being inseparable from the Christian flourishing of the churches he has served (cf. 2 Cor 4:12–15; 1 Thess 3:8):

> I rejoice all the more for myself, hoping to be saved, because I see in you that the Spirit is poured out upon you from the rich well of the Lord. . . . Reckoning that, if I take the trouble over you to impart something of what I have received, my service of such spirits as yours will count towards my reward, I have

hastened to send to you briefly, so that with your faith you may also have perfect knowledge (1.3, 5).

So who was Barnabas? Unfortunately, attempts to locate him geographically and chronologically have so far yielded only conjectures and controversies.

The letter was certainly written after the destruction of the Temple in AD 70, to which it refers (16.4). And it cannot have been written much later than about 170, since it had acquired sufficient renown and authority to be treated as part of the New Testament by Clement of Alexandria in the late second or early third century.[1] Clement cites the letter as being by 'the apostle Barnabas',[2] which almost certainly means that he identified our author with the Barnabas whose story is told in the Acts of the Apostles. The same identification was unambiguously made by St Jerome,[3] but it has found few modern defenders.[4]

The doctrinal affinities of the letter led Prigent quite plausibly to locate our author in Palestine or Syria,[5] but the most that can be proved is that the author's intellectual background is to be sought there, which, in the case of an itinerant teacher, proves little or nothing about where he was working when he wrote his letter or where the church he was addressing was situated.

Though the background to much of what Barnabas writes is Jewish or Jewish Christian, Barnabas dissociates himself entirely from the Jews, to whom he refers as 'them' (in contrast to 'us', the Christians). His great worry is that Christians will be beguiled into Judaizing, a risk which he expresses in terms of 'us' becoming 'proselytes' (3.6), language which would be most natural if at least the recipients of the letter were of pagan extraction. Whether a writer who was himself a convert from Judaism could talk like that is at any rate doubtful.

The early church took shape within the matrix of a Judaism which was much less homogeneous than it became after the devastation of Jerusalem and the destruction of the Temple. Different movements and schools of thought argued, sometimes fiercely, about the correct interpretation of the Law. Not surprisingly, the Christians found themselves joining in this dispute, with their claim or indeed claims to possess true knowledge of God's will. Barnabas is no exception. For him too Christianity is essentially the revelation of God's Law, of the way marked out by God's commandments, whose end is life. Indeed, the short second section of his letter is a version, probably his own adaptation, of the Two Ways, with which we are already familiar. Christians are those who have received 'knowledge of the way of righteousness' (5.4). The crucial point is laid down almost at the beginning of the letter:

> There are three teachings of the Lord: the hope of life (which is what our faith is all about);[6] righteousness (which is what judgement is all about); love, which is the attestation of the joy and exultation of works done in righteousness. (1.6)

Christianity contains a promise (life) and an indication of what the conditions are for the attainment of this promise (righteousness). And it tells us how to recognize that the works commanded by righteousness are being done, as they should be, joyfully.

However, the situation is, as we have seen, more fraught for Barnabas than it was for the Didachist. For the Didachist, with his background in Pharisaism, the revelation of the Law is almost blessing enough. But Barnabas is closer to the more intense atmosphere of Qumran. As we have noted, his version of the Two Ways comes equipped with angelic powers presiding over each of the ways, and the ultimate 'authority' concerned with the way of death is 'the ruler of this present lawlessness' (18.2).

Over and over again in the early sections of his letter Barnabas warns his readers that the times are evil, and there is an enemy always on the look out for some opportunity to 'slip in some error' and so to 'sling us out from our life' (2.10). The remedy, for Barnabas, as it was for the sectarians of Qumran, was constant watchfulness and study.[7] And, just as it was believed at Qumran that the official Jewish cult had been completely overtaken by error, so that it was displeasing to God and tantamount to idolatry, representing, no doubt, a victory for the Angel of Darkness,[8] so in Barnabas's eyes Judaism as such was the typical misreading of God's will; the Jewish Law, as such, was due to a diabolically inspired misunderstanding of God's words (9.4). The first and longest part of the letter is therefore devoted primarily to earnest warnings against being misled 'like them' and to a display of how the Bible ought correctly to be understood.

The Old Testament inevitably put the early Christians in rather a quandary. On the one hand, it provided them with the only authoritative source they had in which to search for clues to the understanding of what it meant to believe in Jesus as the Christ; on the other hand, it contained a Law which, especially after the admission of pagans to the church, they did not expect everyone to follow. It soon became a matter of dispute whether it was even legitimate for

Christians to observe the 'Jewish Law'.[9] The church apparently needed both to affirm and to deny the authority of the Old Testament.

Various attitudes could be adopted in face of this dilemma. St Paul and the author of the Epistle to the Hebrews argued that the Jewish Law had played a legitimate role in the past, but was now superseded by the new covenant in Christ (cf. Rom 7:1-6; Gal 3:23-25; Heb 8, 10). The logic of this position meant that there was really no reason for the church to go on taking any notice of much of the Old Testament. This seems effectively to have been the view of Ignatius: realizing that he was wasting his time arguing on their own terms with people who refused to believe anything they could not find in the Old Testament ('the ancient records'), he dismisses the whole problem with the cry, 'My "ancient records" are Jesus Christ, the records that cannot be touched are his cross and his death and his resurrection and the faith that comes through him' (Phld. 8.2). Ultimately the natural outcome of this position was reached by heretics like Marcion, who denied that there was any role at all for the Old Testament in a religion based on the newness of Jesus Christ.

Another approach exploited the tensions which, as had long been recognized, occur within the Old Testament itself. By playing off texts in the prophets against texts in the Pentateuch it was possible to argue that certain features of Jewish observance, notably the whole sacrificial cult, were never really desired by God. It seems that some Hellenistic Jews were already maintaining this, and they could appropriate Jesus very readily as the reformer they were looking for, who would purge Judaism of its unwanted features. This is the line taken by Stephen in the speech reported in Acts 7.[10]

If bits of the apparent Law were not really meant by God, how did they come to be there in the first place? Various answers were given to this question, all of them, once again, implying that at least parts of the Old Testament were of no concern to Christians. It could, for instance, be maintained that the whole Law was indeed given by God, but, apart from the Ten Commandments, it was all intended simply as a response to Jewish infidelity, either to coerce them into fidelity or to mark them out for condemnation. In this context appeal could be made to Ezekiel 20:24-25, 'Because they did not observe my commandments ... I have given them instructions which are not good and commandments in which they shall not live'.[11]

Alternatively a ploy could be used, which was probably already

25

current in some Hellenistic Jewish circles, to suggest that some parts of the Law were not given by God, but by Moses.[12] More drastically, use could be made of the conventional view that the Law was given by angels (a device no doubt originally meant to safeguard divine transcendence) to suggest that some parts of the Law were interpolated by a wicked angel. This view led to the famous doctrine of 'false pericopae' found in the Pseudo-Clementine Homilies.[13]

Barnabas appears to be aware of several, if not all, of these different ways of coping with embarrassing bits of the Bible, and he is clearly not happy with them. He is concerned both to show that the Old Testament in its entirety is a Christian book and to show that all the essentials of Christian faith and practice are contained in it.

It was, of course, not original to Barnabas to interpret the Old Testament with reference to Christ and his church. Much of his exegesis can be shown to derive from earlier Christian traditions. What is probably original to him is the conviction that the whole Old Testament can be read in a Christian way, so that all of it can be interpreted as applying to Christians, without conceding any ground to the Judaizers.

What Barnabas has undertaken is nothing less than a whole interpretation of revelation, and such an interpretation also highlights, for him, the urgency of his undertaking.

The scope of revelation is all-encompassing. Echoing a phrase which goes back to Homer and Hesiod,[14] he says:

> The Lord, through his prophets, has made known to us the things that are past and the things that are present, giving us also the beginnings of a taste of what is to come. Seeing all of it being made effective, in detail, just as he told us, we ought all the more richly and exaltedly to apply ourselves to the fear of him. And I, not as your teacher, but as one of you, will show you a few things, by which you may have joy in the present situation. (1.7–8)

It looks as if the revelation of past, present and future is linked in Barnabas's mind with the three teachings of the Lord enunciated immediately before this passage.[15] The hope of life, which obviously looks to the future, is based on faith, which looks to the past, to the whole of salvation history (cf. 5.3). Judgement is what the future contains, though the result of taking it seriously is that it makes demands on how we behave in the present. The works done in righteousness clearly belong to the present, but the joy there is meant to be in them comes from having a proper understanding of them in the context of the whole of revelation. It is joy that Barnabas wishes his readers to obtain through his message, and this joy is associated in his mind with wisdom and knowledge (2.3), and it is precisely knowledge that he hopes to impart (1.5). And the love which is the attestation of joy in good works is perhaps to be identified as the love which makes Christians ready to communicate to each other whatever wisdom and understanding they have from God.

There is, however, more to the present and the future than righteousness and judgement. Revelation, as understood by Barnabas, includes an apocalyptic dimension, alerting us to the perilous situation in which the world stands, under the sway of the devil and in imminent expectation of the 'final stumbling block' (4.3). In such circumstances understanding is a necessity, not a luxury (4.5), and it may well be that the resulting joy provides the strength to enable Christians to stand firm and not be led astray under the pressures of the present age of lawlessness and the hazards which are soon to come (4.9).

Although Barnabas does say a certain amount in this vein about the present and the future, he is not confident that his readers can hope to have anything like the same understanding of them as they can of the past. At the end of the main part of his letter he says that he hopes he has missed out nothing of what can be explained simply, but 'if I wrote to you about the present or the future, you would not understand, because it is all in parables' (17.1–2).

The main thrust of the first and longest section of the letter, then, is to explain the past, to offer a way of interpreting the Bible. This should protect Christians from misunderstanding the Law, as the Jews did. And this then leaves the way open for a brief reminder of what the authentic Law is, as formulated in the Two Ways.

Barnabas begins his exposition by showing that God does not want sacrifices. To this end he first quotes Isaiah 1:11–13, adding the comment,

> So he has put a stop to these things, in order that the new law of our Lord Jesus Christ, being without any yoke of constraint, should have as its oblation one that is not of human construction. (2.6)

Talk of the 'new law' appears to accord a certain validity to the 'old law', and Barnabas's other comments here belong in the context of the doctrine that the sacrificial cult was part of the

27

disciplinary code imposed on the Jews because of their infidelity (it was a law of constraint) and the contention that the sacrificial system was man-made. The hint that the new law has a sacrifice which is not man-made is not developed here, but later on it becomes clear that the sacrifice of the new law is the sacrifice Christ made of himself on the cross (5). However, we should not push the phrase 'new law' too far. Although in the Epistle to the Hebrews the 'new covenant' is invoked to show that there was a previous covenant which is now superseded (8.7-13), the Qumran documents also talk of a 'new covenant', without any such implication.[16] And, as we shall see, Barnabas is keen to affirm that the Christians are a 'new people'.

Barnabas now cites a composite 'text', made up of Jeremiah 7:22-23 and Zechariah 7:10 and 8:17, to show that God is properly approached, not with sacrifices, but with morally acceptable behaviour. Composite texts like this derive from primitive Christian accumulations of proof texts ('testimonia');[17] Barnabas seems to have been familiar with several collections of testimonia, and they no doubt influenced his more systematic attempt to claim the Old Testament as a whole for the Christians.

This 'quotation' is followed by the comment,

> So, since we are not without insight, we ought to perceive the will of the goodness of our Father in speaking to us, wishing us to search out how we are to approach him, without being led astray like them . . . (2.9)

This leads straight into another 'quotation', in which a verse from Psalm 51 is combined with a text of unknown provenance, and then there is a final comment from Barnabas:

> So what he says to us is, 'A sacrifice to God is a contrite heart, a sweet-smelling savour to the Lord is a heart which glorifies its Maker'. So we ought to be accurate, brethren, about our salvation, in case the evil one sneaks in some error and slings us out from our life. (2.10)

This is one of several passages where Barnabas contrasts what God says 'to us' with what is said 'to them', and Barnabas's distinctive doctrine is already made clear: whatever he may have appeared to be saying earlier, the Jewish Law never did have any validity, it was nothing but a misunderstanding on the part of the Jews. Christians must make sure, by being 'accurate', that they do not make a similar mistake. A true understanding of sacrifice shows that God never wanted animal sacrifice, he wanted a suitable attitude on our part: that is the authentic sacrifice.

It is worth noting that, on the face of it, Barnabas's concern is somewhat curious. By the time he was writing, the Temple had been destroyed, so the whole sacrificial system had collapsed anyway. So why is Barnabas so earnestly warning Christians to keep clear of it? Whether he has some specific point in mind or whether he is just repeating a bit of traditional polemic, as part of his general campaign against Judaizing, will perhaps become clearer in due course.

There follows a quotation from Isaiah 58, split into a part addressed to 'them', in which the Lord rejects the Jews' practice of fasting, and a part addressed to 'us', revealing that genuine fasting means generous behaviour towards other people. Barnabas concludes this little section with the comment,

> So, brethren, the patient one was looking forward to the way in which the people he had prepared for his Beloved would believe purely, when he revealed it to us in advance about everything, in case we should be shattered against their law like proselytes. (3.1–6)

Barnabas now issues a warning about the times in which he and his readers were living:

> In connection with the present situation, we must seek out with much research the things that can save us. Let us flee perfectly from all the works of lawlessness, in case the works of lawlessness overtake us, and let us hate the deception of this present time, so that in the future we may be loved. Let us not allow our souls to relax, so that they would be free to consort with wicked people and sinners, in case we become like them. The final stumbling block has drawn near, about which scripture speaks, as Enoch says . . . (4.1–3)

As is normal with apocalyptic, the prophecies which follow are difficult to interpret with any confidence. They both appear to derive from Daniel 7:7–8, although Barnabas is clearly under the impression that the first one comes from some other source, apparently Enoch.[18] The development of the passage as a whole gives us at least a fairly clear idea of what Barnabas's purpose is. He is unambiguously warning his readers that the final stumbling block is about to appear on the scene; because of that, 'You ought to understand' (4.5)—meaning, surely, that it is necessary to understand

God's will correctly, not that it is necessary to understand the prophecies. The reference to scripture in 4.3 is most naturally taken to mean that Barnabas is alluding to some canonical or non-canonical description of what the final stumbling block is. Enoch and Daniel are then cited to show that this predicted stumbling block is imminent. If this is correct, then Barnabas himself must be responsible for applying the prophecies to his own time. And this must mean that, if we can crack the prophecies and see what historical situation Barnabas was applying them to, we can on that basis work out the date of his letter.[19]

The prophecies, in a nutshell, state that ten kingdoms will rule on the earth, and then a little king will humble three of the kings in one fell swoop (4.4–5). The most plausible interpretation is still that of Lightfoot:[20] the ten kingdoms refer to Roman emperors. If we include Julius Caesar as the first, the tenth is Vespasian (AD 69–79). The three kings who will all be humbled at once must then be Vespasian and his two sons, Titus and Domitian, both of whom were given the title 'Caesar' during their father's reign.[21] Since in fact both Titus and Domitian succeeded their father quite peaceably, no little king came along to humble them all in one fell swoop, so Barnabas's prophecy was not fulfilled. He must therefore have been writing before the death of Vespasian. What 'little king' he was expecting we can only conjecture, but it is possible, as Lightfoot suggested, that it was some sort of *Nero redivivus*. Nero was the archetypal persecutor of Christians, and it seems that his return from the dead was expected in some circles.[22]

After underlining in this way his conviction that the test of the final persecution is imminent, Barnabas goes on, once more rather in the vein of Qumran, to warn his readers to be attentive and not to 'be like some people, piling up your sins, saying, "Our covenant stands firm for us"'. 'It is *ours* indeed, but *they* lost it for ever, when Moses had already received it' (4.6–7). There follows the story of how the Israelites fell into idolatry while Moses was receiving the law from God on the mountain, and how Moses flung the tablets inscribed by God's finger away from him, so that they broke. 'Their covenant was broken, so that the covenant of the Beloved, Jesus, should be sealed into our hearts in the hope that comes from faith in him' (4.7–8).

The Jews, on this account, never received the covenant at all and, because of their ill-timed indulgence in idolatry, they definitively lost any chance they ever had of receiving it. But this does not mean that Christians can afford to be cocksure. The apostasy of the Jews, after all the wonders they had seen during the Exodus, stands as a warning to the Christians:

> All the time of our life and faith will benefit us nothing if we do not resist, as is fitting for children of God, in this present lawless age and in the coming trials. (4.9)

Barnabas takes this occasion to introduce another of his characteristic themes: it would be a big mistake to think that we are already justified:

> Do not go off on your own, as if you were already justified, but come together and search out what is for your common benefit. (4.10)

Since God is going to judge without respect for persons, exactly on the basis of what each individual has done, we must, as far as we can, 'practise the fear of God and struggle to keep his precepts, so that we may rejoice in his commandments'.

> Let us be on our guard in case, if we relax on the grounds that we have been called, we may go to sleep over our sins and the evil ruler take power over us and drive us out from the kingdom of the Lord. (4.1–14)

Barnabas now launches into an extended and rather confusing discussion of the incarnation and the passion, whose connection with what goes before is apparently this: we must not go to sleep over our sins, because the reason why 'the Lord endured to surrender his flesh to corruption was so that we might be purified by the remission of our sins, which there is in the sprinkling of his blood' (5.1). The immediate moral drawn from this is:

> So we ought to be more than grateful to the Lord, because he has made the past known to us and, in the present, he has given us instruction, and we are not without insight with regard to the future. Scripture says, 'It is not without justice that nets are spread for birds', meaning that it is not unjustly that anyone will perish who has knowledge of the way of righteousness, but still confines himself to the way of darkness. (5.3–4)

The rather miscellaneous points that emerge from this section (5.1 - 6.7) can be summed up in a few clauses which do not, of course, do justice to the somewhat convoluted texture of Barnabas's exposition or the lumps of exegesis it contains. Barnabas makes it clear that the essentials of the incarnation, the passion and even the manner of Jesus' death are all contained in and interpreted by the prophets. Part of the message concerns the people of Israel, part concerns 'us'. What needs to be explained is how the Lord of the world, the one to whom God said at the outset, 'Let us make man in our own image', could bear to suffer at the hands of men. From 'our' point of view, he endured it 'to abolish death and to reveal the resurrection' and to fulfil the promises made to the fathers. He appeared in the flesh because in no other way could human eyes have looked on him—they are, after all, incapable even of looking at the sun, which is only a creature. Appearing in the flesh, the Son of God, preparing 'the new people' for himself, showed that, after bringing about the resurrection, it is he who will be the judge. He revealed himself as Son of God by choosing as his apostles the worst sinners available, demonstrating that he came, not to call the righteous, but sinners. This is the good news—and presumably part of the underlying logic, connecting this disquisition on the incarnation and the passion with what has gone before, is that, if the Son of God went out of his way to make it clear that he had come to call sinners, his 'new people' must not dream of taking their stand on any putative covenant which would assure them of their righteousness. St Paul's objection to Pharisaism in Philippians 3, that it aims at a perfection that can in principle be had now, instead of the righteousness which comes through faith in Christ and which has to be sought as an ever-receding goal throughout this life, is echoed elsewhere in Barnabas's attack in Judaism and can probably be invoked here to explain the sequence of ideas.

For the Israelites, though, the incarnation and the passion are not good news. The Son of God also endured his passion in order to bring to a head the sins of those who had persecuted the prophets. And woe to those who conspired against him!

As Barnabas has already told us, the people of Israel lost the covenant before they ever received it and they lost it definitively. In that sense, they were doomed not to benefit from the coming of Christ. To this extent Barnabas goes along with the exegetical tradition which identified parts of the Old Testament law as designed to mark the Jews out for condemnation and to prevent them from recognizing their Saviour when he came.[23] But it is significant that Barnabas nowhere actually ascribes any such malevolent purpose to any biblical texts. The Jews' failure to accept Christ was the natural outcome of their whole history of infidelity, but it was not, in Barnabas's eyes, actually brought to pass by God's word.

32

The next section of the letter (6.8–19) is a complex bit of exegesis, weaving together the themes of the promised land, the passion and the creation of Adam. Since it is extremely interesting as a piece of doctrine, as well as illustrating the ingenuity with which Barnabas uses the Old Testament, it will be worth examining in some detail.

Barnabas begins by paraphrasing Exodus 33:1–3:

> Behold, thus says the Lord: Enter into the good land, which the Lord promised to Abraham, Isaac and Jacob, and make it your inheritance, a land flowing with milk and honey. (6.8)

This he then interprets as meaning, 'Hope in the one who is to be revealed to you in flesh, Jesus'. This rather startling bit of exegesis is justified on the grounds that 'man is earth that has had something done to it' (*gē paschousa*)—Adam was created from the earth. But the phrase *gē paschousa* is more naturally translated 'suffering earth', and there is no doubt that an allusion to the passion is intended (6.9). So the good land, the land flowing with milk and honey, is to be identified with reference to the incarnation and the passion of Jesus (whose purpose, we remember, was to prepare a new people, purified by the remission of their sins thanks to the blood of Christ).

Barnabas now develops his allusion to creation:

> Having renewed us, then, in the remission of sins, he made us to be a different pattern, so as to have our soul as a child, thanks to him recreating us. For Scripture is referring to us when he says to the Son, 'Let us make man in our image and likeness, and let them rule the beasts of the earth and the birds of heaven and the fish in the sea'. And, seeing our good creation, the Lord said, 'Grow and increase and fill the land'. (6.11–12)

Having established a link between the creation of Adam and the passion of Christ, Barnabas here establishes a link between the creation of Adam and our re-creation in Christ, with the claim that the story of Adam's making is really about us, the Christians.

This last claim is further supported by a non-canonical text of uncertain origin: 'The Lord says, "Behold, I make the last things like the first" ' (6.13). On this basis Barnabas feels justified in saying that this is what the prophet meant, when he said, 'Go into the land flowing with milk and honey and master it'. The fact of our recreation is further substantiated by an appeal to Ezekiel 11:19, inexactly quoted:

> As he says in another prophet, 'Behold, says the Lord, I will take out of them', those, that is, whom the Spirit of the Lord foresaw, 'their hearts of stone and put in hearts of flesh', because he himself was going to appear in flesh and dwell in us. (6.13-14)

This last point is then developed with reference to a composite citation apparently derived from Psalm 42:2 and Psalm 22:22, showing that 'the dwelling-place of our heart is a holy temple for the Lord' (6.15-16).

The triumphant conclusion of this remarkably devious exegesis is that we are the ones who have been led into the 'good land' (6.16). The suffering humanity of Christ is simultaneously the land to which we have been called and the genuine fleshliness which is at the heart of our recreated human nature. Our entry into this promised land is the fulfilment of the purpose expressed by God right at the beginning, to make man in his own image and likeness.

What then of the milk and honey? A young child is fed first on honey, then on milk (6.17). We have already been told that, as a result of the forgiveness of our sins, we have a soul which is like a child, so it is not difficult to apply this to ourselves: 'So we too, being made alive by faith in the promise and by the word, shall live, mastering the land' (6.17). But remember what it says in Genesis: 'Let them grow and increase and rule the fish'. And who, Barnabas asks, 'can now rule the beasts or the fish or the birds of heaven?' (6.17-18).

> We ought to perceive that ruling belongs to authority, so that someone is master when he gives a command. So, if this does not happen now, then he has told us when it will happen: when we too are made perfect to become heirs of the covenant of the Lord. (6.18-19)

The land we have entered, then, flows with milk and honey because this is the food of children, and we are children. But we must grow up before we can master the land. We are not yet perfectly heirs of the covenant. As we have been warned, we are not yet justified.

It seems indisputable that Barnabas is here exploiting for his own purposes a Christian tradition of interpreting the Genesis story on the assumption that Adam was created as a child.[24] What is novel is his further suggestion that the whole story in fact refers to us and our (re)creation in Christ, which itself depends on an identification between the earth from which Adam was created, the promised land

and the suffering humanity of Christ. This brilliant (if, by modern standards, perverse) bit of exegesis contributes importantly to the demonstration of Barnabas's pet theses, that the Old Testament as a whole is about Christ and his new people, and that it is a big mistake, typified by Judaism, to claim to be further advanced towards perfection than we really are.

The next section of the letter (7 – 8) takes up the hint dropped earlier on and shows how the self-oblation of Christ on the cross is what the ritual of the Day of Atonement and the sacrifices for sin prescribed in the Bible and developed in Jewish liturgy are all about.

The details of Barnabas's commentary are far from limpid, perhaps partly because he knew more about the Jewish ritual than we do. But it is clear that Barnabas wants to claim that what the Lord had in mind from the outset, in issuing his instructions about the Day of Atonement, was his own future sacrifice of his own flesh, which had been adumbrated even earlier by the sacrifice of Isaac (7.3, 5). There can therefore be no question of seeing even the minutiae of the rite as deriving from a secondary law, intended to discipline the Jews, or from any interpolation by Moses or a wicked angel. The whole thing rests fully on God's authority and has its meaning only with reference to the events of Good Friday. The goat that was sacrificed on the Day of Atonement, the scapegoat and the sacrifices offered for sins all really signify the self-oblation of Christ.

The sacrifice of the new law, we recall, is one which is 'not of human construction' (2.6), and Barnabas appears to be looking for features of the rituals under discussion to bear this out. He begins his account of the Day of Atonement by remarking that, in spite of a precept threatening death to anyone who breaks the fast, the priests, and they alone, are commanded to eat of the sacrifice. Since he inserts into the middle of this observation a reference to the Lord himself offering the sacrifice of 'the vessel of the Spirit' and to his fulfilment of the 'type' of Isaac,[25] it is possible that Barnabas means us to see the priests as foreshadowing Jesus' own consigning of himself to death. The priests, in the Jewish ritual, are apparently condemning themselves to death by not fasting, even if it is out of obedience to another precept. On the other hand, their adding vinegar to the sacrificial meat foreshadows their role in bringing Christ to his passion: although (and Barnabas reiterates the point) Christ offered the sacrifice of himself, it was at their hands that he suffered and they gave him vinegar to drink.

In the case of the scapegoat it is the whole people that is involved, and Barnabas assures us that at the judgement they will say, 'Is not this the man we mocked and pierced and spat on and crucified?'

In the case of sin-offerings, Barnabas points out that those who bring the heifer (meaning Jesus) to slaughter are grown men, but after that there is no further role for them, 'there is no further glory for sinners'. The people who sprinkle the assembly, so that everyone may be cleansed from sin, are 'children' (signifying the apostles sent out to purify hearts by preaching the gospel).

Barnabas seems to be insisting both on the role of the Jews in killing Jesus and on the fact that it was he himself who achieved the sacrifice and the ensuing purification. If we imitate the Jews' mistake by Judaizing, we run the risk of identifying ourselves with the crucifiers of Jesus, and so overlook the true priest who offered the sacrifice, and so cut ourselves off from benefiting from it.

The real meaning even of the non-biblical details is entirely Christian, but the Jews, of course, cannot understand this: 'These things ... are clear to us, but obscure to them, since they did not hear the Lord's voice' (8.7). This gives Barnabas his cue to explain why they did not hear the Lord's voice, and this turns on the correct understanding of circumcision.

The circumcision that was intended all along was a circumcision of ears and hearts. 'He circumcised our hearing, so that we might hear the word and believe' (9.4). The circumcision in which 'they' have placed their confidence has been brought to nothing: what God commanded was not circumcision of the flesh, 'but they transgressed, because a wicked angel instructed them' (9.4). This 'wicked angel' is reminiscent of the Qumranian 'Angel of Darkness', but it is possible that Barnabas is already reacting to a doctrine like that found later in the Pseudo-Clementine homilies, attributing undesirable bits of the Bible to diabolical interpolation. At any rate, Barnabas's position is clear: the Jewish understanding of the Law is and always was mistaken. Properly understood, the Law always did mean something other than what they have taken it to mean.

Barnabas then tackles the dietary regulations in the Bible, which, he says, are 'not a commandment of God not to eat, but Moses was speaking in Spirit' (10.2). This evidently echoes the tradition that some of the commandments were added by Moses, but Barnabas is not interested in exploiting it to discredit the dietary laws. The Jews, he says, were beguiled by their 'carnal lust' into applying literally to food the prescriptions which Moses meant spiritually (10.9). Psalm 1 shows what Moses really intended: in telling people to abstain from certain kinds of fish, meat and fowl, Moses was actually making a moral point, as the Psalmist understood:

> Blessed is the man who has not walked in the counsel of the impious (like fish which walk in darkness in the deeps). Nor has he stood in the way of sinners (the people who seem to fear the Lord and sin like pigs). Nor has he sat on the seat of plagues (like birds which settle down to plunder). (10.10)

This sums up an extended allegorical interpretation of some of the dietary rules telling people what they may not eat (10.3–8). Then follows a brief section on the rules telling people what they may eat:

> Moses said, 'Eat everything that is cloven-hoofed and chews the cud'. What does this mean? . . . Cleave to those who meditate the distinctions involved in the word they have received in their hearts, and to those who declare and observe the commandments of the Lord, and to those who know that meditation is a joyful work and who chew the cud of the Lord's word. And what does 'cloven-hoofed' mean? That the righteous person walks in this world and looks forward to the holy age. See how well Moses legislated! (10.11)

It was precisely so that we might understand all this that the Lord 'circumcised our hearing'; but there was no way in which 'they' could understand, having fallen at the first hurdle, thanks to the wicked angel who made them misunderstand circumcision, so that their hearing remained uncircumcised (10.12).

In the next section of his letter Barnabas appears to change direction. So far he has been concerned chiefly to show that Jewish observance rests on a misunderstanding of the Bible, which should be understood as referring to Christ and his new people. Now he seems more interested in showing that the Old Testament contains all the essentials of Christianity: 'Let us look and see if the Lord took the trouble to make a revelation in advance about the water and the cross' (11.1). A variety of texts is cited to show that the Old Testament does indeed tell us about baptism, the cross, the crucifixion and Jesus (11–12).

On baptism, Barnabas contrasts the Jews, who have 'erected a baptism' for themselves, which cannot bring remission of sins, with the Christians, who are 'like a tree planted by the water-courses, which will yield its fruit in due season, and its leaves will not fall' (Psalm 1).

See how he designated together the water and the cross. What he is saying is this: happy are those who have gone down into the water, hoping in the cross. In saying 'in due season' he means: I will give him his reward then. As for now, 'its leaves will not fall', meaning: every word which comes from you through your mouth in faith and love will serve to convert and bring hope to many. (11.6–8)

Further, rather imprecise, scriptural texts elicit the further explanation:

We go down into the water full of sins and filth, and we come up bearing fruit in our hearts, having fear and hope in Jesus in our spirits. 'And whoever eats of them will live for ever.' This means: whoever hears these people speaking and believes will live for ever. (11.9–11)

It is worth noting the role of words in Barnabas's view of Christianity. Christians can look forward to receiving their reward 'then' (at the end), but what is given now is the removal of sins and fruitfulness in speaking. We are reminded of the love which is the attestation of the joy there is in works of righteousness (1.6). We are not yet justified or perfect heirs of the covenant, but we should have the kind of charity which makes our faith reach out to others in words, and the effectiveness of such words is, perhaps, the essential way in which we already have a foretaste of what is to come (1.7). This is certainly the gospel according to a minister of the word!

After discussing a few more texts, in which he triumphantly discovers the doctrine of the cross, the crucifixion and the divinity of Jesus (12), Barnabas then turns to the covenant: 'Let us see if it is this people or the first one that is the heir and if the covenant is for us or for them' (13.1). Barnabas argues on the basis of Genesis 25:21–23, 48:11–20 and 17:5 that it is the 'younger' people that is designated as the heir, and that the promise to Abraham was that he would be the father of nations of uncircumcised believers (13.2–7). The episode of the Golden Calf is then cited for the second time, to show that God did indeed give the covenant to the Israelites, but their sins made them unworthy to receive it. So 'Moses received it, but they were not worthy' (14.1–3).

Moses received the covenant, but only as a servant. It was to *us* that the Lord himself gave it (14.4).

He was manifested so that they might be brought to completion in their sins, and that we might receive the covenant of the

> Lord Jesus through him who is the heir, who was made ready
> for this very reason, that, appearing in person, he might rescue
> from darkness our hearts which were already consumed by
> death and delivered to the lawlessness of error, and place the
> covenant in us by his word. (14.5)

We notice that the primary heir is in fact Jesus; it is through him that
we become heirs of the covenant. His humanity is the promised
land, from which we are created; only our 'creation' means our
deliverance from death and error.

Various texts from Isaiah are then cited to prove that God
appointed his Son to be a covenant and a light for the nations and to
bring salvation to the ends of the earth (14.6-9)

Barnabas then turns to the Sabbath. As he points out, the
commandment to hallow the Sabbath day is contained in the Ten
Commandments (15.1), which ought to cause problems to anyone
claiming that the Ten Commandments are an eternally valid law,
unlike the secondary or interpolated laws. As cited by Barnabas, the
commandment says, 'Hallow the Lord's Sabbath with clean hands
and a pure heart'. Commentators have suggested that this wording
of the precept may derive from some tradition of spiritualizing the
commandment,[26] but Barnabas does not, this time, contrast a correct spiritual interpretation with an incorrect Jewish interpretation.
Instead he explores what is meant by the Sabbath. 'God made the
works of his hands in six days and he finished on the seventh day and
he rested on that day and hallowed it.' With the help of Psalm 90:4,
Barnabas shows that this means that 'the Lord will bring all things to
an end in 6,000 years'. So the seventh day is 'when his Son comes
and puts a stop to the time of the lawless one and judges the impious
and changes the sun and the moon and the stars; then he will properly rest on the seventh day' (15.3-5). So the Sabbath belongs to the
end of time, which we have not yet reached. Barnabas has already
reinterpreted the creation of Adam eschatologically; here he extends
the process to creation as a whole. Creation is still in the making, so
there is, as yet, no Sabbath to celebrate.[27]

The same point is then made in another way. The commandment
calls for the hallowing of the Sabbath 'with clean hands and a pure
heart'. 'So', Barnabas comments, 'if anyone is pure in heart and can
now hallow the day which God has hallowed, then we are completely
mistaken about everything.' Otherwise, God himself will rest and
hallow his Sabbath when we ourselves will be able to hallow it,

having first been made holy ourselves, and that will not be until we have been justified and have received the promise, when lawlessness is no more and everything has been made new by the Lord (15.6–7). The mistake of the Jews, once again, is to have assumed that we are further along the way than we really are.

In the meantime, we celebrate the eighth day, on which Jesus rose from the dead and ascended into heaven. And this is appropriate, because the Sabbath which God has made is the one on which he will bring all things to their conclusion and make a new beginning, the beginning of a new world, of an eighth day (15.8–9).

Finally Barnabas takes up the question of the Temple. 'They' have misguidedly pinned their hopes on a building, just like pagans, when, as Isaiah 40:12 (taken with 66:1) shows, God does not dwell anywhere (16.1–2). Barnabas then cites an unknown prophecy to the effect that 'Those who have destroyed this Temple will themselves rebuild it', a prophecy which, according to Barnabas, is now in the process of being fulfilled. The Temple has already been destroyed by the enemies of the Jews, and 'now the very servants of their enemies will rebuild it' (16.3–4).

This prophecy has tempted some scholars to try to identify some specific project for rebuilding the Temple which Barnabas might have had in mind, but the results are all highly dubious—and it is more prudent in any case to note that here, as in 4.3–5, we are dealing with a prophecy which interests Barnabas because it is already half fulfilled; there is no reason to look for any historical occurrence to which the unfulfilled part applies.

Lightfoot suggested that the rebuilding of the Temple by the servants of the enemies who destroyed it should be seen as signifying the new, spiritual Temple, the church of Christ, built by Christians who are loyal subjects of the Roman empire,[28] but Barnabas is surely referring to the rebuilding of the Temple which was destroyed, not some other Temple; nor is there any reason for him to regard the building of the spiritual Temple as being in the future (in 16.6–10 he shows precisely that there is now such a Temple). Nor is there any point in Barnabas identifying the Christians as servants of the Romans; if we interpreted 4.3–5 correctly, Barnabas views the Roman empire as hostile, or likely to become so, to the Christians.

Whatever Barnabas's prophecy originally meant, if we take it at its face value, as he cites it, it means that the Temple in Jerusalem is going to be rebuilt by the Romans or their servants. And this must surely imply some unholy alliance between the Romans and the

Jews.[29] If this is correct, the prophecy in 16.3-4 must be taken in conjunction with that in 4.3-5, as indicating a peril that is about to break upon the church. Barnabas could surely see the restoration of the Temple only as a threat, and, if he seriously believed that the Temple was going to be restored, with the backing of the Romans, that might well explain why he regards the temptation to Judaize as the most dangerous temptation facing the church in these last days when the 'final stumbling block' is about to appear. And it is not totally absurd to suppose that Christians in the 70s could have had such a nightmarish vision of a Jewish–Roman conspiracy against them. The archetypal persecutor of Christians was Nero, and there is some reason to believe that it was partly at the instigation of the Jews that he launched his persecution, even if it is unlikely that the theory ascribing Jewish interests to his wife Poppaea has any historical foundation.[30]

Whatever we make of the prophecy and its interpretation, there can be no doubt that, in Barnabas's eyes, any restoration of the Temple would achieve nothing except the repetition of a fundamental mistake. God never did want that sort of Temple.

Is there then any Temple at all? There is indeed, and it is one built by the Lord himself 'on the name of the Lord' (16.6).

> Before we believed in God, the dwelling-place of our heart was corruptible and weak, truly a temple made with hands, because it was full of idolatry and it was a house of demons, because we did everything that is opposed to God. But 'it will be built on the name of the Lord'—pay attention to this—so that the temple of God may be built 'gloriously'. How? Listen. When we received remission of our sins and hoped in the Name, we became new, being created again from the beginning. So God truly dwells in us in our dwelling-place. How? His word of faith, the invitation of his promise, the wisdom of the commandments, the precepts of doctrine, he himself prophesying in us, he himself dwelling in us leads into the incorruptible temple those who had been enslaved to death, by opening for us the door of the temple, which is the mouth, giving us repentance. For anyone who desires to be saved does not have regard for the human person, but for him who dwells and speaks in the human person. (16.7–10)

This somewhat complicated explanation of the true nature of the 'spiritual Temple being built for the Lord' (16.10) picks up themes we have already met, particularly that of the word which is spoken for the benefit of others. Barnabas sees a close connection between the repentance that is given to us and the indwelling of God in us precisely in the form of prophesying in us, so that the door of the Temple (our mouth) is opened and others who were enslaved to death can receive through us the word that will save them.

Barnabas has now reached the end of the first and most substantial section of his letter. By the use of typological exegesis, numerology, allegory and eschatological reinterpretation, he has shown us how to read the Old Testament as a Christian book, so that we will be able to resist the allurements of Judaizing. The task is, of course, not complete. He has not interpreted every word of the Bible. To put up the necessary resistance in the evil days ahead, the church must continue to study assiduously. But, in principle, Barnabas has disarmed the Jewish threat and, in the process, he has also disarmed any doctrine which would effectively or explicitly deny the authority of all or parts of the Old Testament or its application to the Christian church.

No doubt Barnabas's most important message is his way of reading the Bible, but he has also given us a coherently eschatological view of Christianity, dramatically opposed to the misguided complacency which he finds typified in Judaism. We have been given a new beginning, and can strive to keep the commandments of God, but we are not yet justified, not yet perfect; we do not yet have clean hands and a pure heart. What we do have is hope, hope focused on the cross of Christ. We also have words; because we have an anticipatory share in what is to come, we can speak effectively to one another, for each other's salvation. Instead of being side-tracked by false assurance into splendid isolation or into futile cultic observances, we meet together and engage in a common research into God's word, generously speaking whatever words we have for one another's benefit. And so we proceed along the way of life.

So 'let us turn to another knowledge and teaching' (18.1). Thus does Barnabas introduce his own version of the Two Ways. Granted his belief that the two ways are 'ways of teaching and power' (18.1) and that the odds are stacked in favour of the wrong side, it is not surprising that he adds various items to the received text to bolster up our commitment to the way of life. He totally ignores the original structure of the catechesis and simply produces a string of precepts and exhortations, but this procedure allows him to highlight at the outset the importance of making a real commitment and the motives which induce such commitment. The first precept, to love God, is expanded into a threefold exhortation:

> You shall love him who made you, you shall fear him who formed you, you shall glorify him who rescued you from death. (19.2)

This picks up two motives Barnabas has alluded to in his letter: fear of God (1.7) and gratitude to him (5.3, 7.1). Then, instead of going on to the second commandment, of fraternal love, Barnabas continues:

> You shall be simple in heart and rich in spirit.
> You shall not adhere to those who walk in the way of death.
> You shall hate all that is not pleasing to God.
> You shall hate all hypocrisy.
> Do not abandon the Lord's commandments. (19.2)

Most of the material in Barnabas's Two Ways corresponds to what we find in the *Didache* and the *Doctrina*, however much it is rearranged. But there are some little touches which Barnabas has apparently added, which tally with the message of his letter. Thus he bids us to be pure, for the good of our soul, 'as far as you can' (19.8), which reflects his conviction that we are not yet pure. And the uncertainty of our condition is brought home to us with the exhortation, 'You shall remember the day of judgement night and day' (19.10). Typical of Barnabas's religion of the word is his encouragement to us to apply ourselves to atoning for our sins either by 'toiling in words' or by doing manual work (19.10).

The letter concludes with conventional exhortations and requests for prayers, but we may notice how, to the end, Barnabas refuses to play the 'teacher' in any way which would reduce either the responsibility of the individual Christian or the role of God:

> Be good lawgivers for yourselves, remain faithful counsellors of yourselves. . . . May God, the Lord of all the world, give you wisdom, insight, understanding and knowledge of his commandments. Be taught by God, searching out what the Lord wants of you, and do it, so that you may be found on the day of judgement. (21.4–6)

It would be absurd to claim that Barnabas is one of the great theologians of the early church; but, bumbling as he sometimes is, and disconcerting as he usually is to a modern reader, it would be unfair not to recognize the significance of his message. Particularly important, in the long run, was his attempt to show that the church can and should appropriate as its own the whole of the Old Testament. The church could not go on simultaneously appealing to the authority of the Old Testament and denying that much of it had any application to Christians. No book can be expected to function as sacred scripture on that basis.

So who was Barnabas? We have seen reason to date the letter to the 70s, which makes it possible for it to have been written by the Barnabas mentioned in the New Testament. Granted the accumulating evidence of Jewish hostility to the Christians, it is not hard to believe that the man who disappointed Paul by aligning himself with the Judaizers about AD 50 (Gal 2:13) should by the 70s have come to believe in the radical incompatibility of the two religions. The only question is whether even then he could have talked about 'us' becoming 'proselytes' (3.6). 'Barnabas' seems not to have been a common name; perhaps it was only a nickname anyway (Acts 4.36); we should therefore not seek refuge in the possibility of our letter being by someone else of the same name. The ascription to 'Barnabas' must mean an ascription, right or wrong, to the New Testament Barnabas. And, in spite of the difficulty of 3.6, it is tempting to believe that the converted Levite, who spent some time as one of the 'prophets and teachers' in the church at Antioch (Acts 13:1), who later travelled with St Paul and then quarrelled with him, and who blotted his copy book, in some eyes, by being cowed into Judaizing, is the same man as the teacher who was so concerned in the 70s to warn people against the temptation to which he had once succumbed himself. The question remains open; at least it should not be closed against the traditional ascription being correct.

Notes

1 Eusebius, *Hist. Eccl.* 6.14.
2 *Strom.* II 6.31.2, 7.35.5.
3 *De Viris Illustribus* 6.
4 It is, however, defended by J. D. Burger, 'L'Enigme de Barnabas', *Museum Helveticum* 3 (1946), pp. 180–93.
5 P. Prigent, *L'Epître de Barnabé I–XVI et ses Sources* (Paris, 1961), p. 219, and in his introduction to the Sources Chrétiennes edition (Paris, 1971), pp. 22–4.
6 Literally, here and in the next phrase, 'the beginning and end of our faith . . . the beginning and end of judgement'.
7 Barnabas's insistence on 'searching out' (*ekzētein*) God's command-

ments (e.g. 2.1, 21.6) recalls the Qumranian insistence on *midrash* (etymologically equivalent to *ekzētein*) (e.g. 1QS V, 11–12; VIII, 15–16; G. Vermes, *The Dead Sea Scrolls in English* [Harmondsworth, Middx, 1975], pp. 79, 86); in particular his concern for 'accuracy' in these dark days (2.10) echoes CD VI, 14 (Vermes, p. 103). Cf. also 1QH II, 31, 'You have saved me from the zeal of lying interpreters' (Vermes, p. 156).

8 Cf. Vermes, pp. 42–6. 1QH IV seems to identify the cult actually being practised in the Temple with idolatry (Vermes, pp. 161–2). For the Angel of Darkness, see 1QS III, 18–21 (Vermes, pp. 75–6).

9 The dispute was in full swing in the second century (cf. Justin, *Dial.* 47), but its origins lie much earlier, in the dispute between those who saw Christianity as reforming Judaism from within and those, most notably St Paul, who wanted Christianity to be quite separate (cf. the very plausible thesis put forward by F. Watson in *Paul, Judaism and the Gentiles* [Cambridge, 1986]). As early as the *Didache* at least some people thought that it was wrong for Christians to associate themselves with Jewish observance (*Did.* 8).

10 Cf. M. Simon, 'Saint Stephen and the Jerusalem Temple', *Journal of Ecclesiastical History* 2 (1951), pp. 127–42. There may even have been a current in Palestinian Judaism sympathetic to this view; it is remarkable that Rabbi Johanan ben Zakkai, who emerged as the leader of Jewish thought after the destruction of the Temple in 70, argued that Judaism had now outgrown the need for animal sacrifices (cf. E. M. Smallwood, *The Jews under Roman Rule* [Leiden, 1981], pp. 346–7).

11 Ezekiel is quoted to this effect in Justin, *Dial.* 21.4, and in the *Didascalia* (trans. R. H. Connolly [Oxford, 1929], p. 230). Justin argues that circumcision was a sign marking out the Jews for punishment (*Dial.* 16.2, 92.2–3). Cf. in general Connolly, *op. cit.* pp. lvii–lxix.

12 Philo, *Vita Mos.* 190, *Decal.* 175 (cf. F. T. Fallon, 'The Law in Philo and Ptolemy: A note on the Letter to Flora', *Vigiliae Christianae* 30 [1976], pp. 45–51); Rabbinic orthodoxy rejected this view (Sifre Num. 112; *Everyman's Talmud*, pp. 145–6). The ascription of part of the Law to Moses is found, for instance, in the Clementine Recognitions I, 36 and Irenaeus, *Adv. Haer.* IV, 15.2.

13 Cf. G. Strecker, *Das Judenchristentum in den Pseudoklementinen* (Berlin, 1958), pp. 166–87; Strecker brings out the derivation of this doctrine from Jewish exegetical embarrassment at some features of the Bible.

14 *Iliad* I, 70; Hesiod, *Theogony* 38. Cf. W. C. van Unnik, 'A formula describing prophecy', *New Testament Studies* 9 (1963), pp. 86–94. J. Reiling, *Hermas and Christian Prophecy* (Leiden, 1973), pp. 77–9, shows that, as here, the use of this formula tends to go with the claim that prophecies about what is now past can be seen to have been correct, from which we are to infer that the prophecies about what is still future are reliable too.

15 1.7 is introduced by *gar* ('for'): 'there are three teachings of the Lord, *for* the Lord has made known to us . . .'.

16 Cf. Vermes, pp. 35–8.

THE APOSTOLIC FATHERS

17 There are important studies of the testimonia by Prigent, *L'Epître de Barnabé I-XVI*, and J. Daniélou, *Etudes d'Exégèse Judéo-chrétienne* (Paris, 1966). There is some evidence of similar compilations at Qumran (cf. Vermes, pp. 245-9).

18 The syntax of 4.3-4 should probably be interpreted to make 'as Enoch says' in 4.3 look ahead to 'he says thus' in 4.4. For a similar interruption between the first 'he says' (or equivalent) and the account of what is said, this latter being introduced by a resumptive 'he says' (or equivalent), cf. 2.9-10 and 5.2.

19 The prevailing orthodoxy is that this passage can be used only to date Barnabas's source, not Barnabas himself (cf. Prigent in the Sources Chrétiennes edn, p. 26); but this does not explain why Barnabas cites the prophecy. One would hardly seek to instil a sense of urgency by quoting in 1989 a prophecy of the imminent end of the world in 1969. J. A. T. Robinson, *Redating the New Testament* (London, 1976), pp. 313-19, argues for taking 4.3-5 at its face value and suggests an early date for the letter.

20 J. B. Lightfoot (ed.), *The Apostolic Fathers* (London, 1893), pp. 240-1.

21 This is affirmed by Dio Cassius 65.1, and it is confirmed by the evidence of coins (cf. Lightfoot, *loc. cit.*).

22 The evidence is given in L. W. Barnard, *Studies in Church History and Patristics* (Thessalonica, 1978), p. 68; but I do not find Barnard's argument in favour of a later dating of Barnabas convincing.

23 According to the *Didascalia* (*ed. cit.*, p. 222), Deut 21:22-23 was intended precisely to make the Jews incapable of recognizing Christ; that the text did genuinely pose a difficulty is shown by Justin, *Dial.* 89.2.

24 Although it is not attested as such before Barnabas, there is no reason why it should not already have been traditional to say that Adam was created as a child. Cf. Theophilus II, 24-25; Irenaeus, *Adv. Haer.* IV, 38; Clement of Alexandria, *Protr.* 111, *Strom.* III, 103.1; Ephrem, *Hymns on Paradise* 11.1. Jerome evidently regarded this as a point on which Christians disagreed with the Jews (*Epitaphium Paulae* 25.3).

25 By this time it was probably generally believed that Isaac voluntarily accepted death, when it looked as if he was going to be sacrificed: cf. J. Bowker, *The Targums and Rabbinic Literature* (Cambridge, 1969), pp. 231-3.

26 Cf. Prigent *ad loc.* in the Sources Chrétiennes edition.

27 Cf. the very similar move made by Christ in John 5:17.

28 *Op. cit.*, p. 241.

29 This is not as impossible as it might seem. The destruction of the Temple in 70 seems to have been only an incidental feature of the sack of Jerusalem, not a matter of deliberate policy; and the reorganization of Judaism at Jamnia after the destruction of the Temple went on with the blessing of the Romans (cf. Smallwood, *op. cit.*, pp. 346, 349-51).

30 Cf. Smallwood, pp. 217-19. On Poppaea, see Smallwood, 'The alleged Jewish tendencies of Poppaea Sabina', *Journal of Theological Studies* NS 10 (1959), pp. 329-35.

3

Hermas 1: The Visions

The *Shepherd* of Hermas, judging from its geographical allusions (e.g. Vis. 1.1, 1.1–2; 4.1, 22.2), is a Roman work, and according to the Muratorian Canon it was written 'recently', while its author's brother, Pius, was Bishop of Rome (i.e. between *c*. 142 and *c*. 154), but there are grave reasons for doubting the reliability of this testimony, and a date in the late 60s or in the 70s seems more plausible.[1]

The picture Hermas gives of himself in the *Shepherd* is almost certainly not genuinely autobiographical; he seems to have adopted a literary persona for didactic purposes. But it is probably true that he was not an official of the church. As we learn from him, the church he was addressing (presumably the church in Rome) was governed by presbyters (Vis. 2.4, 8.3), and he appears not to be one of them. Deacons are also mentioned, as are teachers and prophets, but Hermas himself seems not to fit into any of these categories. He presents himself as having received a succession of visions, in which he was commissioned to write a message to the whole church in the neighbourhood. He was himself to read it 'to the city', and he was to send copies to Clement, who was responsible for 'the towns outside' (that is, neighbouring towns regarded as belonging to the same church), and to Grapte, who was evidently the lady in charge of widows and orphans (ibid.). Whether he actually had these visions or whether he simply used them as a literary device, it is impossible to say, and it makes almost no difference to our understanding of what he wrote.

The book, as we have it now, is divided into three sections, though this may not quite correspond to its original structure. First there are five 'visions', then comes a series of twelve 'commandments', and last there is a long section consisting of ten 'parables'.

The Visions give us a lively picture of Hermas (or his literary persona) as an ex-slave (1.1, 1.1) who has become quite prosperous (3.6, 14.7), but who suffers from a nagging wife and a ghastly brood of spoiled children (2.2, 6.3; 1.3, 3.1). Because he has failed to bring them up properly, they have ruined him with their sins (1.3, 3.1). They have even betrayed their parents in some way (2.2, 6.2), though apparently not by denouncing them to the authorities as Christians, since Hermas is not counted among those who have suffered for their faith (3.1, 9.9). Things have got so bad that Hermas is inclined to leave his wife and to give up any attempt to be reconciled with his children (2.3, 7.1).

Nevertheless, in spite of his dismal external circumstances, Hermas is introduced as a notoriously cheerful and good-tempered man (1.2, 2.3), morally upright and devoid of malice and duplicity (1.2, 2.4). His religion is sincere and seemingly untroubled. As he travels about the district he admires God's creation and gives glory to its Maker (1.1, 1.3), and he turns easily to prayer and to confessing his sins (ibid.; 3.1, 9.5–6).

What relationship there is between the author's real personality and his literary persona it is unprofitable to consider, but the picture is well drawn and 'Hermas' comes clearly before us as one of those inoffensive religious people who preserve their good humour by keeping themselves to themselves, even if this does mean abandoning their responsibilities rather lightly. They are genuinely moral, but with little moral sensitivity. They find it easy to confess their sins, because they do not do anything that really shocks them; as a result, they are rather helpless in face of the much worse behaviour of other people. Their very harmlessness makes them unlikely to be the victims of persecution. There is little to stop them getting through their whole lives in benign ineffectiveness.

Hermas, however, was stopped. His story begins—and it is told with considerable narrative skill—with his renewed acquaintance with the lady who had owned him as a slave. Without preamble, he tells us 'The man who raised me sold me to a lady called Rhoda in Rome. Many years later I recognized her and began to love her as a sister' (1.1, 1.1). Then one day he saw her bathing in the Tiber and helped her out of the river. 'Seeing her beauty, I thought in my heart, "How happy I would be, if I had a wife like that, of such beauty and manner".' And he insists, 'That was all I thought, and nothing else' (1.1, 1.2).

48

The episode did not strike him as particularly significant until, some time later, when he was walking to Cumae, he fell 'asleep' and was taken in spirit to a desolate place, where he saw heaven opened and Rhoda appeared to him in heaven, claiming that she had been assumed there 'to denounce your sins to the Lord', and assuring him that God was angry with him. He protests that he has never said an improper word to her: 'Have I not always thought of you as a goddess? Have I not always respected you like a sister?'

Rhoda laughs, and in the context there is something rather sinister about her laughter. Goddesses caught bathing are dangerous beings, and none the less so if they laugh. She reminds him of his having desired her. 'Does it not seem to you a wicked thing for a righteous man, if a wicked desire enters his heart?' And she leaves him in no doubt about the consequences of such wickedness: 'People who plan evil in their hearts are clutching death and captivity to themselves, particularly if they are people who make much of this world and exult in their wealth and do not keep a firm hold on the good things which are to come. They have no hope and have despaired of themselves and their life and their souls will regret it.[2] But you, for your part, must pray to God and he will heal your sins and those of all your household and of all the saints' (1.1, 1.3–9).

Hermas is terrified and wonders how he can be saved, if even such a modest sin of thought is going to be taken into account (1.2, 2.1).

So far Hermas has not put us in the picture about his dreadful family. The sin which precipitates his first shock is therefore seen simply as a sin in the mind against chastity, and Hermas discovers with horror that a far more exigent standard of personal morality is required than he had suspected.

This first lesson, however, though it is not false, turns out to be beside the real point. The heavens close up again and Rhoda is seen no more, but now Hermas finds himself confronted by an old lady sitting on a comfortable white chair, who asks him why he is not his usual cheerful self. He tells her.

The old lady confirms that sins of thought are serious. Desiring evil comes as a terrible shock to 'an entirely holy and already tested spirit' (1.2, 2.2–4). Nevertheless, this is not why God is angry with Hermas; it is because he wants him to call his unruly children to heel. Hermas's misguided love for his children has allowed them to become fearfully corrupt. But God has had mercy and will give him strength, so: 'Just do not be remiss, but be of good heart and strengthen your household'. 'A daily righteous talk overcomes all wickedness.' And, the old lady assures him, 'I know that if they

49

repent with all their heart, they will be enrolled in the books of life with the saints' (1.3, 3.1–2). She then reads him what is evidently a terrifying apocalyptic account of the impending judgement, which ends, however, on a more reassuring note: God will make the way easy for his elect, so as to give them the promise he has made, provided they 'keep the commandments of God in great faith' (1.3, 3.3). As she is carried away by two attendants, she tells Hermas, 'Be a man' (1.4, 4.3).

A year later (2.1, 5.1) Hermas meets the old lady again, and this time she is walking about. She gives him a message 'to God's elect', which he copies out 'letter by letter', since he finds it all unintelligible (2.1, 5.3–4). After a fortnight of prayer and fasting, the meaning is revealed to him, and it turns out, rather surprisingly, that the message is mostly addressed to Hermas personally and concerns his family again. They are now revealed to be even worse than we had realized. His children have run the whole gamut of wickedness, and his wife is guilty of not restraining her tongue. But all the sins they have committed to date will be forgiven, if they repent whole-heartedly and eliminate all undecisiveness (*dipsychia*, literally 'two-souledness') from their hearts. There is still time, though it is a limited time, for the 'righteous' (presumably meaning 'the Christians') to repent. The Gentiles, on the other hand, can repent any time up to the last day (2.2, 6.1–5).

Then comes a message to the leaders of the church to 'set their ways straight in righteousness', and then, seemingly, all Christians are exhorted to persevere in righteousness without dithering. 'Blessed are all of you who endure the coming great tribulation and do not deny your life. The Lord has sworn by his Son that those who deny their Lord are disinherited from their life, those, that is, who are going to deny him in the days to come. Those who denied him previously will find him gracious to them in his great compassion' (2.2, 6.6–8).

Then Hermas is told not to leave his wife, and to change his attitude to his children. He has been unforgiving towards them, letting his behaviour be dictated by the remembrance of their offences. Such an attitude, he is told, results in death. Instead, he must try to educate and discipline them aright, so that they can be 'cleansed from their former sins'. And, because of his negligence, he himself is implicated in their sins. What has saved him so far is his 'not abandoning the living God', his straightforwardness (*haplotēs*, simplicity) and his great self-control, qualities that will save everyone who 'walks in innocence and simplicity' (2.3, 7.1–2).

As an appendix to this second Vision, a 'most beautiful young man' (obviously an angel) appears to Hermas some time later in his sleep and asks him who he thinks the old lady is who gave him the message. 'The Sibyl', he replies. The angel explains that it is the church, and she is old because she was the first of all to be created, and it was for her sake that the world was made (2.4, 8.1).

Going to the place appointed for his next assignation with the old lady, Hermas finds an ivory bench there, with a linen cushion and a linen covering. Feeling terrified, he starts trembling and his hair stands on end, but, coming to himself, he kneels down and begins to confess his sins according to his normal practice (3.1, 9.4–5). The old lady arrives and listens to him praying and confessing his sins. Then she touches him and tells him to stop always praying about his sins; he should also pray about righteousness, asking to receive a share in it for his household (2.1, 9.6).

Hermas begs the lady to show him the vision she had promised him before, and he sees a great tower being built out of shining, square stones. It is being built 'on water'. The six young men who attend the lady are the actual builders, but thousands of others bring them stones from various places. Some of the stones are accepted, while others are rejected (3.2, 10.4–9). As we learn from the explanation which Hermas extracts from the lady, the tower which he can see being built 'is I myself, the church' (3.3, 11.3). It is built on water because 'your life was saved and will be saved by water' (3.3, 11.5). The reference to baptism is unmistakable, but there is also probably a reference to the creation, when God 'founded the earth upon the waters' (1.3, 3.4). The tower, like the heavens, is securely established on the Word of God (ibid.; 3.3, 11.5). If the whole world was created for the sake of the church, the church herself is, in a way, the 'real' world. The six young men who are building the church are the six first-created angels, who have been made responsible by the Lord for developing and building 'the whole creation' (3.4, 12.1), which confirms the identification between the church and creation. If the purpose for which the world was created is that the church should be built, then naturally the angels responsible for bringing the world to its fulfilment set about doing so by erecting the 'tower' of the church.

Several points of interest emerge from the interpretation of the different kinds of stone. The primary building-blocks, which fit together perfectly, are apostles, *episkopoi*, teachers and deacons 'who always agreed with each other and kept peace with each other and listened to one another'. Other stones which are used immediately, without needing to be dressed, are those who have suffered for the name of God and those who have walked the straight path of the Lord's commandments. An interesting group (which apparently does need some stone-dressing, though this is not said explicitly) consists of those who are 'young in the faith and faithful'; because there is no malice in them, they are admonished by the angels and encouraged to do good. These are not necessarily newcomers to the faith, but they are people whose faith is at the same time innocent and rather immature—which is more or less the situation of Hermas, as he has depicted himself. Though they fall short of full righteousness, they possess an essential quality of childish guilelessness which wins them the paedagogical attention of the angels (3.5, 13.1–4).

The rejected stones fall into various classes. There are sinners who want to repent, so they are not thrown far away from the tower. If they repent while the tower is still being built, they will be 'strong in faith' and serviceable for the building, but if they leave it too late they will remain rejects, though they will have the privilege of 'lying near the tower' (3.5, 13.5).

Some stones are smashed and then flung far away from the tower; these are people who pretend to believe, without giving up any of their wickedness, thereby incurring the wrath of the Lord (3.6, 14.1).

A lot of stones are lying around, which cannot be used in the building. Some of them are pock-marked; these are people who recognized the truth, but did not persevere in it or cleave to the saints (3.6, 14.2). No doubt they are to be identified as people who never actually repudiated Christianity, but, because they consorted chiefly with unbelievers, drifted away from the faith which they theoretically acknowledged to be true.

Then there are cracked stones, people who bore grudges against each other and refused to be at peace, keeping malice in their hearts, in spite of putting on a friendly appearance (3.6, 14.3). Some stones are mutilated; these are people who believe and keep to righteousness on the whole, but retain some element of 'lawlessness' (3.6, 14.5). Other stones are the wrong shape for the building because, though they are beautifully white, they are round. They are people who have faith, but also have wealth, and in time of persecution they deny their Lord for the sake of their worldly prosperity. They will become good for the building when the wealth which enchants them is trimmed. Hermas himself is cited as a case in point: now that he has lost at least some of his wealth, he is 'profitable from the point of view of life' (3.6, 14.5–7).

Of the stones which were thrown away and not just left lying around, some rolled off the road into the wilds; these are believers who continued to dither and doubt and so left the true path, looking for a better one. Other stones fell into the fire; these are people who went the whole way in abandoning God because of their bad desires, that it never even occurred to them to repent. Some stones fell near the water, but were unable to roll into it; these are people who wanted to be baptized, but were then frightened by the moral demands of the truth and changed their minds (3.7, 15.1–3).

Hermas asks whether all these stones which have been thrown away can repent, and he receives the surprising answer that they can repent, but cannot be built into the main tower, only into a much smaller tower elsewhere, and that only after they have 'been tormented and have fulfilled the days of their sins'. Provided they then acknowledge their faults, they will be transported from their torments because of their 'share in the righteous Word'. Otherwise, if they do not acknowledge their faults, their hardness of heart will prevent them from being saved (3.7, 15.5–6).

It is the privilege of apocalyptic to be obscure, and it is vain to look for a clarity that such literature is not intending to provide. But we can at least try to grasp what Hermas's story is telling us. It does not seem that the relegation of some stones to a second tower is due to the completion of the first tower: the distinction is clearly significant between the stones which are left lying around and those which are thrown away, and this primary division is established while the tower is still being built.

The possibility of repentance is apparently open to everyone (except perhaps the pseudo-believers, the stones that were not merely thrown away, but smashed). But the consequences of repentance are different in different cases. The stones that are lying around can be built into the main tower, whereas those which were thrown away can only be built into the second tower. The significant feature of the first category seems to be that the genuineness of the faith of the people concerned is not called into question; it is their practice which is defective. Even in the case of the wealthy who deny their Lord, the problem is one of practice, not belief. The stones which are thrown away, on the other hand, are people who cannot decisively make up their minds to be believers. They keep on wondering whether there is not some better philosophy of life than Christianity, or they throw themselves so whole-heartedly into their sinful delights that there is no longer even any tension between their moral practice and the moral ideals of the gospel, so that effectively they have decided to leave Christian belief out of account; or else they cannot quite bring themselves to undertake the Christian life in the first place, so decide not to get baptized after all. These are people who are not even trying to be Christian. And the best hope that can be offered them is to let them run the course of their wickedness and learn, belatedly, when they have to pay the price for it, that ʾ͵ were at fault. Their repentance is not a fruitful conversion to a ιι͵ way of life, but simply the recognition of their previous faults. And it is remarkable that even on that basis they can be saved, though only with a kind of second-class salvation.

The possibility of a second-class salvation is alluded to elsewhere in some early Christian writings,[3] and it dramatizes the optimistic belief we have already met in the *Didache* that it is worth doing what we can, even if we fall short of perfection. But in Hermas the generosity of salvation is extended in a rather different way, to embrace people who were not even trying to be serious Christians, who could not make up their minds to accept Christianity as true until it was too late to do anything about it. This presumably reflects, benignly and realistically, a situation in which there were all sorts of people on the fringe of the church, whether baptized or not, who were fascinated by Christianity but could not bring themselves to make any real intellectual or moral commitment to it. Hermas's message is surprisingly tolerant towards them, as it is towards people driven by their own worldliness to deny the Lord. The ideals remain high and, in the last analysis, stringent; but mercy will not despair until it has to.

It should be noticed that Hermas is here concerned only with believers, with people who, in some sense or another, appear to be attached to the church. And, unless they repent, many of them will turn out not to belong to the church after all. This is where the stringency comes in. But it is a nuanced stringency. First of all, faith is a requirement of a quite different order from anything else. People without a genuine commitment to the faith are not even in the running for inclusion in the tower of the church, whatever consolation prizes they may be eligible for. And the only people who are not only rejected, but rejected angrily and smashed, are those whose faith is a mere pretence. On the other hand, those who are 'young in the faith' receive preferential treatment: even though their Christian practice is evidently not perfect (which is why they need to be admonished and corrected by the angels), they are already built into the fabric of the church, unlike others whose virtue is defective. These people are young precisely in being devoid of malice (cf. Mand. 2, 27.1) and in having total confidence in God—unlike those who have grown old in their woes because they did not cast all their cares upon God (Vis. 3.11, 19.3). They have a kind of innocence which renders even their failings almost innocuous (cf. Sim. 9.31, 108.2). They are people like Hermas, at least as he presents himself (Vis. 2.3, 7.2), and a major part of his book consists precisely of the admonitions he received from his angelic mentor. It is particularly interesting that, when he returns to the imagery of stones at the end of the *Shepherd*, the 'round' stones, representing people who are too rich (like Hermas) and who need to be cut down to more modest prosperity (not to poverty, be it noted), are described as a 'race of innocents', none of whom will be lost (Sim. 9.30–31, 107.4 – 108.2).

The structure of Hermas's Christian ethics is further explicated in a revelation of seven 'women' who have the responsibility of 'carrying' the tower. They are, it transpires, seven virtues, arranged in a genealogical sequence, so that each is the mother of the one that follows. In order, they are: faith, self-control, straightforwardness, innocence, decency, knowledge and charity (Vis. 3.8, 16.2–8). These foundational virtues represent the proper Christian attitude, from which the whole array of Christian behaviour arises.

Within Christian behaviour, a certain emphasis is placed on peace and concord within the church, an emphasis which is reinforced by the very image of the tower, in which evidently it is necessary that the stones all fit together. And this emphasis is underlined in the concluding message which the Church gives Hermas to deliver to everyone: after complaining about the wickedness of her 'children', she says, 'So now listen to me and be at peace among yourselves and visit and support each other. Do not keep to yourselves too lavishly the things that God has made, but share them with those who are in need' (3.9, 17.1–2). After rebuking first the self-indulgent rich and then the presbyters, she returns to the theme of peace at the end of her communication:

> So, children, see to it that your dissensions do not deprive you
> of your life. How do you propose to discipline the Lord's elect,
> if you have no discipline yourselves? So discipline one another
> and be at peace among yourselves, so that I may stand cheer-
> fully before the Father and give an account of you all on your
> behalf to your Lord. (3.9, 17.9–10)

As the old lady departs at the conclusion of the third vision, Hermas clamours to have one more point explained to him: when she first appeared to him, she looked very old and infirm. The next time she

55

looked rather more sprightly and was standing up. The third time she was marvellously beautiful and young-looking (3.10, 18.2–5). After fasting for a day, Hermas receives a vision in the night, in which an angel, with some show of reluctance, provides the explanation he was wanting. The lady's appearance reflected the changing state of the church. The first time, 'your spirit was old and already worn out, having no strength because of your softness and indecisiveness'. But, after the first revelation of the Lord's compassion, 'your spirits were rejuvenated and you put away your softness and strength came to you and you were fortified in the faith'. What has happened to the church is like what happens when an old man, who has given up hope because of his frailty and poverty, suddenly learns he has received an inheritance: he gets up and his spirit is renewed and he 'becomes a man' again (3.12, 20.2–3).

After the message of the second vision, assuring everyone of the possibility of repentance, the church was even more invigorated, like someone who had been miserable receiving good news. And the bench Hermas saw in the third vision, standing solidly on its four feet, represents the solidity of the world, secured by its four elements: 'So those who repent completely will be young and well-founded, if they have repented whole-heartedly' (3.13, 21.1–4).

As has already been remarked, Hermas's story cannot be taken as mere autobiography. There are sufficient incongruities in it to alert us to the fact that even the anecdotal sections are meant to make a point, not just to give us the news. Respectable ladies like Rhoda did not bathe in the Tiber, where they could be seen by any casual passer-by, for one thing. And it is difficult to believe in Hermas's children. Why should the lady, who is the Church, address a public message to all Christians, most of which is about Hermas's own family? His 'children' are surely the same as the people she addresses as her children, the whole Christian community.

It is proper, then, to look for hints as to the meaning of the whole story, not just its explicit messages to the church. And one such hint is surely contained in Hermas's supposition that the old lady who appears to him is the Sibyl. To anyone thinking in pagan terms in Rome, she would no doubt be the obvious candidate; but should Hermas be thinking in pagan terms? The pagan elements in the story of Rhoda have often been noticed and have sometimes surprised commentators. But surely they are deliberate. She represents the apotheosis of an essentially pagan ideal of perfection and her diagnosis of Hermas's fault is more wrong than it is right. It is true that

Hermas should not have desired her, but that is not why God is angry with him. His more significant fault is that he has neglected to discipline his family. It is only when the story moves on from Rhoda that we are allowed to see what lies behind Hermas's passing thought that she would make a lovely wife: he already has a wife and she is so awful that Hermas is thinking of leaving her. It is easy to love the ideal Rhoda as a sister, but what the Church tells him is that his wife is going to be his 'sister' (2.2, 6.3). Whether or not this means that in future they are going to live together in continence, it signifies at least that it is to her that he must look for Christian companionship.

Rhoda is introduced as the lady who had bought Hermas as a slave, and she shows few signs of mercy. But she is perfect like a goddess, and she appears to Hermas in heaven. Of course she is a tempting and impressive alternative to his wretched wife. But no sooner has she disappeared than the authentic agent of revelation appears, the Church. And she is, at first sight, far less impressive. She is an old lady, sitting snugly in her armchair, and she is definitely on this earth. There is nothing of the nymph caught bathing about her. And, unlike Rhoda, she is thoroughly human even though, it transpires, she is the first of all creatures. Unlike pagan perfectionism, the church has become thoroughly incarnate, and her incarnation is the actual church, made up, on the whole, of rather unsatisfactory believers. If Hermas was tempted by Rhoda, but was forced to return firmly to his family, this surely dramatizes a sort of conversion from an essentially pagan ideal of personal virtue to an ecclesial virtue, in which it is important to remain united with the disappointing and annoying multitude. Pagan ethical standards, as found in most philosophical schools, are not necessarily wrong, but they are incomplete and lead to a misjudging of human situations, not least because paganism could not know that the whole world exists for the sake of the church, so that incorporation into the church must be the goal which interprets all one's life. Nor could paganism accept the principle of incarnation, which Hermas alludes to, with characteristic apocalyptic indirectness, in his presentation of the church as both the first of all creatures and as an all too human society.

Hermas's temptation, then, needs to be rediagnosed as a temptation to disown the church. It is not so far removed from the fault of those who would not commit themselves to the faith because they kept on looking round for some 'better way'. In the historical context, the 'better way' would almost certainly be one learned from some sort of philosophical idealism or pagan religiosity. And this is not the last time in Hermas's book that we shall meet this temptation.

Once again, it turns out, we find in Hermas, in a slightly different form, the problematic with which most of the Apostolic Fathers confront us. It is the ecclesial dimension of Christianity which makes it such an unsatisfactory religion, and its unsatisfactoriness has to be accepted on the basis of a radical belief in God's promise, with its attendant commandments. Indecisiveness may indeed be caused by a reluctance to accept Christian moral standards; but it may also be due to misplaced idealism, which finds itself cramped and frustrated in the Christian church. But if the church is the very goal of creation, and the church is incarnated in the actual Christians who surround us, what are we to do?

Hermas at any rate accepts his responsibility within the church and becomes the bearer of God's message to his people. It is a two-edged message. It is certainly a call to all Christians to improve their behaviour, and the initial warning that even sins of thought are formidably serious is never rescinded. But the essential message is, nevertheless, one of hope. It is, above all, an assurance to those who had despaired of their life that they can still repent, whatever their past sins may be. And evidently the message had some effect in rejuvenating the spirits of the faithful. As we learn later on, there were some teachers in the church who maintained that no further repentance was possible after baptism (Mand. 4.3, 31.1). From the very circumspect way in which Hermas deals with this issue, it looks as if it had come to be or was coming to be a widely accepted teaching in Rome that there was no postbaptismal forgiveness for sin, a position which can probably be connected with the doctrine of the Epistle to the Hebrews (itself probably a Roman document): 'It is impossible for those who have once been enlightened and tasted the heavenly gift, and become partakers in the Holy Spirit, and tasted the good word of God and the powers of the age to come, to be renewed again to repentance if they have fallen and to recrucify the Son of God for themselves' (Heb 6:4–6). Hermas's angelic interlocutor diplomatically declares that the rigorist teaching is quite correct. 'After you have received the forgiveness of your sins, you must sin no more, but live in holiness.' But Hermas's ruthless questioning, so the angel goes on, calls for a clarification: recent or future converts must not be misled, because for them there is no further repentance possible, once their past sins have been forgiven. But the Lord has granted a second chance to people who were baptized before 'these present days'. There is therefore a kind of 'jubilee', allowing fallen Christians one opportunity to repent again. Hermas rejoices at this news: 'Listening to your precise explanation I have come back to life, because I realize that if I do not add to my sins I shall be saved'. Whether there is any hope beyond this very circumscribed offer of pardon is left highly doubtful, though it is not entirely ruled out: 'If someone keeps on sinning and repenting, it is of no profit to someone like that; it will be difficult for him to live' (Mand. 4.3, 31.2–7). Even so, 'difficult' is not the same as 'impossible'.

The limit set to the possibility of postbaptismal repentance may seem harsh, and it certainly looks as if Hermas's view of the requirements for salvation is stricter than what we have found in the *Didache* or in Barnabas. Nevertheless, it is clear that his message was intended to be, and was received as, good news. It is not the limit that he is preaching, but the repentance. Contrary to what the rigorists were saying, he is telling fallen believers that there is still a chance for them to be saved. It it seems ungenerous to offer them only one further chance, it should be borne in mind that Hermas believed there was not much time left anyway: the building of the tower will soon be finished (Vis. 3.8, 16.9). And there can be no question of offering anyone a second chance of postbaptismal repentance, when they had previously not even been offered a first chance. And there is bound to be a deadline of some kind; the only puzzle is why the deadline is set before rather than at the end of this life (or the end of the world).

Hermas's attitude to the rigorists is, on the face of it, deferential. But maybe we can see a hint of a more critical stance, if we read between the lines. After all, the position of the rigorists is uncomfortably close to that of Hermas himself, tempted to abandon his ghastly family and dreaming of an idealized wife like Rhoda. The church, as he is obliged to recognize, is far more tolerant than he is, and she shows up his remorselessness as more pagan than Christian. Should not the same be said of the rigorists? They are right to set high standards, as Rhoda was right. But they have underestimated the mercy and the patience of God, and they have left out of account the positive value of incorporation into the church.[4]

Running through the first three visions there is a kind of subplot precisely about Hermas's relationship to visions. At first, the visions simply occur, out of the blue. But in the second vision Hermas receives a letter which he cannot make out, so he fasts for fifteen days and prays for an explanation (2.2, 6.1). The third vision is also procured by fasting and prayer (3.1, 9.1). It is the vision of the tower being built, and Hermas does not know what it means, so he pleads with the lady Church, 'What is the good of my seeing this and not knowing what it is all about?' (3.3, 11.1). The lady rebukes him mildly, or at least teases him, before giving the desired commentary: 'You are an unscrupulous fellow, wanting to know all about the tower' (ibid.). And, more seriously, she tells him to stop bothering her for revelations. 'These revelations are finished. They are complete. But you will not stop asking for revelations, because you are devoid of shame' (3.3, 11.2).

After the explanation of the tower, Hermas confesses to the reader that he was enthusiastic for visions, so he gladly accepted the lady Church's offer to show him something else. This time, he sees the seven 'women' by whom the tower is carried. At the end of this revelation he asks whether it is now time for the end of all things, which provokes an outburst from the lady Church: 'Idiot,' she says, 'can you not see that the tower is still being built? . . . But it will soon be finished. Now do not ask me anything more. This reminder is enough for you and for the saints.' The Church also insists, 'This revelation was not made for you alone, but so that you could show it to everyone in three days' time. You yourself must first understand it' (3.8, 16.9–11).

Hermas still will not give up. As the lady Church is departing, he asks for an explanation of why her appearance has been successively younger each time he has seen her. She refuses to answer, saying that he must ask someone else (3.10, 18.2). Later, that night, she relents enough to appear to him in a dream and tell him that 'every request calls for humility. So fast, and you will receive what you are asking for from the Lord.' He fasts for a day and then an angel appears to him, who asks, 'Why do you keep on begging for revelations in your prayer? Make sure you do not damage your flesh with all these requests. These revelations are enough for you. Can you endure stronger revelations than you have already seen?' (3.10, 18.6–8). Evidently the fasting involved in seeking revelations is becoming a threat to Hermas's health, and he risks seeing more than he could bear.

Anyway, Hermas says that he wants to know why the church seemed to be getting younger. The angel retorts with a generalized complaint, not confined to Hermas (it is expressed in the plural): 'How long will you go on being stupid? But your indecisiveness makes you stupid, and the fact that you do not hold your hearts towards the Lord.' Hermas meekly replies, 'All the same, we shall understand these things more precisely from you' (3.10, 18.9–10). Hermas gets his explanation, but the point by now is fairly clear: if he and his fellow Christians were straightforward enough in their faith, they would not keep on clamouring for this sort of super-natural enlightenment.

The point is developed more fully later on, when Hermas is again badgering his guardian angel for an explanation and is rebuked for being so stubbornly insistent on asking questions. Hermas pleads that if he does not understand what is revealed to him, he will learn nothing. The angel retorts, 'Anyone who is a servant of God and has his Lord in his heart asks *him* for understanding . . . people who are too lazy to pray keep putting off asking the Lord . . . But you have been strengthened by the glorious angel and you are not lazy, so why do you not ask the Lord for understanding and get it from him?' (Sim. 5.4, 57.2–4).

On both occasions Hermas is told not to ask for revelations. If there is any need for him to be shown something, it will be revealed without his asking (Vis. 3.13, 21.4; Sim. 5.4, 57.2).

Once again, Hermas is dramatizing in his own persona an attitude which looks plausible, but is in fact wrong. As we learn from the eleventh Commandment, on true and false prophets, this constant quest for supernatural answers is a product of uncertainty in faith, and it leads people to look for pagan-type oracles (Mand. 11, 57.2–4).[5] It is therefore a variety of the temptation to wander off the true path, looking for a better way. A genuine prophet does not answer questions; in him the Holy Spirit speaks 'when God wants him to speak' (ibid., 43.8).

Hermas has to learn not to try to force revelations by fasting and clamouring for answers. But the revelations he has received were made to him precisely to provide instruction and encouragement for ditherers and doubters. There were people far better than Hermas, who had a much better right to receive visions (Vis. 3.4, 12.3). But Hermas presents himself as embodying precisely the education which he claims he has been charged to communicate to the church. He was the typical decent, but unsound, believer, who needed to be recalled to a real strength in believing.

The fourth vision shows that the lesson has been heeded, more or less. Hermas is walking along the Via Campana, still asking the Lord for a completion of the visions he has already received, 'to strengthen me and bring repentance to his servants who have been tripped up, so that his great and glorious name might be glorified'. Hermas then passes to thanksgiving, evidently feeling quite pleased with himself. But he hears a voice bidding him not to doubt, and while he is wondering what should make him doubt after all the glorious things he has seen, he suddenly notices a dust cloud in the distance. As the cloud grows, he realizes it is something out of the ordinary, and finally an immense monster appears, spitting out fire. Hermas begins to weep and beg the Lord for deliverance, but then he remembers that he has been told not to doubt:

> So, brethren, arming myself with faith in God and remembering the great things I had been taught, I boldly gave myself to the beast. The beast was coming at such a pace that it could have destroyed a city. I approach it, and the huge monster stretches itself on the ground, doing no more than stick out its tongue. It did not move at all until I had passed it. (4.1, 22.3-9)

Shortly after this the lady Church appears walking along the same road, dressed as if for a wedding. She congratulates him on his escape. As she explains to him, because he cast his worry upon God and believed 'that you cannot be saved by anything except the great and glorious name', and because he did not lose faith at the sight of the monster, the angel in charge of beasts was sent to seal the monster's mouth. So now Hermas must tell the Lord's elect that the great tribulation is coming:

> So if you prepare yourselves and repent whole-heartedly and turn back to the Lord, you will be able to escape it, if your hearts are pure and blameless and you serve the Lord blamelessly all the remaining days of your life. . . . Believe in the Lord, you doubters, believe that he can do all things and he turns aside his anger from you and he sends scourges upon you who doubt. (4.2, 23.1-6)

This world, we are told, must perish in blood and fire and the elect will be purified like gold in the fire, provided they stand firm (4.3, 24.3-4). Hermas must never stop warning the saints about the coming great tribulation; 'but if you want, it will be nothing' (4.3, 24.6).

The fifth vision is really a prelude to the next section of the book, the Commandments. Hermas's guardian angel appears to him as the 'shepherd' to whom he has been entrusted, to recap the preceding visions and dictate a set of commandments and parables, which he is to read repeatedly (presumably in public). The angel is also identified as 'the angel of repentance', and Hermas tells his audience that if they abide by the commandments and parables, they will receive everything that the Lord has promised; but if they do not repent at his message, but go on adding to their sins, they will receive just the reverse (5, 25.1–7).

Notes

1   Against the traditional dating, we may notice the following points:

(1) If the Muratorian Canon was composed, as it purports to have been, soon after the pontificate of Pius I, then, when Irenaeus visited Rome *c.* 175, it must have been known that Hermas was a recent writer, in which case, as the Canon points out, his book cannot be apostolic or scriptural. But Irenaeus quotes the *Shepherd* as scripture (*Adv. Haer.* IV, 20.2).

(2) We learn from Hermas that the church is governed by presbyters, with no mention of a single bishop at its head (Vis. 2.4, 8.3; these presbyters are probably not distinct from the *episkopoi* mentioned in Vis. 3.5, 13.1). If this reflects the situation in the middle of the second century, it is strange that Irenaeus could so soon afterwards be confident of the succession of bishops in Rome (*Adv. Haer.* III, 3.3).

(3) If Hermas was writing in the 140s or 150s, it is extremely odd that there is no mention of the heresies of Valentinus or Marcion.

So, even apart from general doubts about the credentials of the Muratorian Canon, its testimony on Hermas is suspect. If we disregard its testimony, there is nothing to stop us dating Hermas much earlier (cf. J. A. T. Robinson, *Redating the New Testament* [London, 1976], pp. 319–22), and there are good reasons for preferring an early date:

(1) The church in Rome had clearly been undergoing persecution fairly recently when Hermas was writing, and worse was expected; this would fit the period after the Neronian persecution after the great fire of AD 64.

(2) The undeveloped theology and ecclesiology of the *Shepherd* suggest an early date.

(3) The influential teachers mentioned by Hermas as denying the possibility of postbaptismal repentance can perhaps be related to the Epistle to the Hebrews, which seems to imply such a doctrine in 6:4–6, and which is commonly dated to the time of the Neronian persecution. By contrast they are difficult to accommodate in a church which could issue the kind of exhortations to repentance which we find in the Letter of Clement. This means that either they appeared after the Letter of Clement was written or they had already been defeated by then, perhaps thanks to Hermas. And they are surely easier to fit in at an earlier date, when the church in Rome was less united (cf. F. Watson, *Paul, Judaism and the Gentiles* [Cambridge, 1986], pp. 88–105).

If Hermas is dated to the late 60s or early 70s, there is nothing to prevent us agreeing with Origen's surmise (PG 14:1282) that the author of the *Shepherd* is the Hermas mentioned in Romans 16:14. Similarly the Clement mentioned in Vis. 2.4, 8.3, could well be the Clement who later penned the Roman letter to Corinth.

2   *Metanoēsousin*: This could be translated 'will repent', but Rhoda seems to be offering Hermas a better prospect than these worldly types. Hermas does not confine the word *metanoeō* to a good sense (cf. Vis. 3.7, 15.2–3; Mand. 11, 43.4), and the variants here in 1.9 show that the word was not taken in antiquity as meaning 'repent' here. For its application to useless regret, cf. Justin, *I Apol.* 52.9.

3   Cf. Ephrem, *Hymns on Paradise* 1.16–17, 10.14. The idea was taken up into some schools of Gnosticism: cf. Clement of Alexandria, *Exc. Theod.* 61.8; Heracleon, frag. 13 (in W. Foerster, *Gnosis* I [Oxford, 1972], pp. 166–7).

4   There is a passage in the Eighth Parable which could be read as making this criticism of the rigorists explicit, and this is how I took it in *Ways of Imperfection* (London, 1984), p. 7, but I now think I was wrong. One class of sinners is described as consisting of 'hypocrites who introduce different doctrines and mislead the servants of God, particularly those who have sinned, by not allowing them to repent and by convincing them of their own foolish doctrines' (Sim. 8.6, 72.5). The parallel between this text and Sim. 9.19, 96.2–3, makes it likely that these are teachers who disallow repentance by denying that there is any need for it, producing doctrines to suit the whims of sinners, purporting to show that their sins are not really sins.

5   On this Commandment, see J. Reiling, *Hermas and Christian Prophecy* (Leiden, 1973).

4

Hermas 2: The Commandments and the Parables

The Commandments, in a rough and ready way, elaborate the genealogy of virtues we have already encountered in the Visions. Hermas has more than one 'checklist' of virtues (that in Sim. 9.14, 92, is not the same as that in Vis. 3.8, 16), so he is clearly not working with a rigid system, but there is a general coherence in his ethical doctrine. The virtues he is interested in are much the same as those we find emphasized in Jewish writings, reflecting not just a common heritage shared by Jews and Christians, but also the fact that the problems facing the Christian community in a pagan environment were much the same as those which confronted the Jews. The identity of the community, indistinguishable as the Christians were, in many ways, from their non-Christian neighbours, had to be maintained by a firm commitment to the faith and to the discipline entailed by the faith. The cohesion of the community had to be safeguarded by the cultivation of Christian society and particularly by the practice of almsgiving and mutual support, and by the avoidance of the sort of conversation that undermined mutual esteem and good will. The unpopular virtue of chastity needed to be specially commended. Trust between fellow believers was to be fostered by a spirit of frankness and simplicity, issuing in ungrudging generosity towards other people. Good humour was more important than bravado, though real courage might always be called for, since the threat of persecution was always there in the background.

The Commandments abandon the scheme of genealogy and instead show us how various virtues belong together in clutches. The first clutch gathers round faith, which is the first and primary precept: belief that there is one God, who made everything out of nothing and who 'contains everything and is alone uncontained', naturally results in the fear of God, and that in turn motivates self-discipline, which leads to the avoidance of all wickedness and the practice of all virtue. In a sense, therefore, this first commandment, if undertaken seriously, is all that is needed (Mand. 1, 26.1–2).

The second clutch of virtues is assembled under the heading of 'simplicity'. 'Have simplicity and be innocent, and you will be like babes that do not know the wickedness which destroys human life' (2, 27.1). The first subordinate virtue in which simplicity is exercised is not speaking ill of anyone or enjoying listening to people speaking ill of anyone, and above all not to believe what is said at other people's expense. Such talk is an 'unsettled demon . . . keep away from it and you will always have good relationships with everyone' (2, 27.2–3). Later on we learn that speaking ill of people is a consequence of inner uncertainty (*dipsychia*) (Sim. 8.7, 73.2). Although the connection is not spelled out, it is clear enough that uncertainty about oneself makes one suspicious of others, and inner dividedness makes for outward dissensions between people. Inner simplicity (or 'singleness') and innocence, by contrast, instinctively believes the best about other people and is distressed by unfriendly talk.

Next, decency (*semnotēs*) is recommended. The Greek word is difficult to pin down precisely. It often carries a meaning close to 'chastity', but Hermas treats of chastity separately, using a different Greek word. Originally it means something more like 'being dignified'. In the context here it must refer to the sort of natural dignity and decency which results from inner integrity and straightforwardness. According to Hermas it makes everything 'plain and pleasant' (2, 27.4).

Thirdly, under the same heading of 'simplicity', uncritical generosity to the needy is called for. The moral is one we have already met in the *Didache*: give to everyone, without wondering to whom you should give and to whom you should not give. The onus is on the receiver, not the giver, to justify the gift in the sight of God, so the giver can give 'simply': 'Do some good work and give simply to all the needy a share in what God gives you as a result of your labours' (2, 27.4–6). The connection is more explicit this time, and in any case it is not hard to see how Hermas moves from simplicity in general to simplicity in almsgiving.

The theoretical substructure underlying this clutch of virtues is one we shall be meeting again, especially in Ignatius and *2 Clement*.

The kingdom of God, according to a well-known apocryphal saying, is associated with the two becoming one:[1] both internal (psychological) and social divisions are to be overcome, and one consequence of this is the disappearance of that undue consciousness of sexuality which resulted from the Fall. Both prudishness and prurience can be replaced by an easy and untroubled 'decency', leaving the way clear for all social relationships to be governed by frankness, trust and practical generosity.

The author of *2 Clement* makes a direct connection between the two becoming one and truthfulness (2 Clem. 12.3). It is not surprising that Hermas's third commandment likewise concerns truth: 'Love truth and let all truth proceed from your mouth'. In this way 'the Lord who dwells in you will be glorified, because the Lord is true in his every word' (3, 28.1).

Hermas presents himself as being deeply distressed, when he hears this, and wonders whether he can be saved. 'In all my life', he confesses, 'I have never spoken a true word.' It becomes clear that it is a very particular kind of truth which is in question, though. What Hermas means is that he has not been honest in his self-presentation, letting people believe that he was a better man than he really was (3, 28.3). Now that he has learned what is required, his angelic mentor assures him, he is to observe it 'so that even the falsehoods you spoke before in your dealings with people, now that these things' (apparently meaning 'what you say now') 'are found true, may also become faithful' (3, 28.5). Commentators have been puzzled over this remark, but it is clear what it means, provided we bear in mind what sort of truth is being talked about. There is no question of lies in general being retroactively turned into truth, nor is Hermas simply being offered the hope that people will forget that he has lied in the past. On Hermas's own account, no one knew he was lying in the past. The point is simply that, if he mends his ways now, he will be validating the impression he gave previously, so that his past self-presentation, even if it used to be false, will no longer be deceptive, so that no harm will have been done by the previous dishonesty.

Truthfulness, in the rather restricted sense envisaged here, is an obvious corollary of the reconciliation of inner and outer, which is part of the process whereby the two become one. The simplicity and innocence commanded in the second precept lead naturally to frankness in one's self-presentation. The Fall led Adam and Eve to hide. Redemption allows them to come out of hiding.

The fourth Commandment deals with chastity, another virtue which is closely linked with the overcoming of internal and external divisions. Hermas links it explicitly with 'decency', which we have seen to be part of 'simplicity'. As we should expect, chastity means refraining even from unchaste thoughts and desires, let alone unchaste practices (4.1, 29.1–3). But the point Hermas wishes to clarify most concerns divorce. If a man's wife commits adultery and he knows about it, he becomes guilty too if he goes on living with her; if she persists in her infidelity, he must put her away. But if he then marries someone else, he commits adultery too, and the same thing applies to a wife whose husband is unfaithful. But if the unfaithful spouse repents and wants to resume the marriage, it is sinful to refuse to take him or her back. That is why remarriage after divorce is forbidden. The servants of God have one chance to repent again—this is the real point of Hermas's whole message—and that chance would be denied if separated spouses were allowed to contract new marriages (4.1, 29.4–9). Exactly the same procedure is to be followed in the case of that other infidelity, for which the Old Testament had already used the metaphor of sexual infidelity, namely idolatry or any other form of paganism; and here too remarriage is forbidden, because the possibility of repentance must be kept open (4.1, 29.9–10).

It is worth noting that there is not the slightest hint in all this that marriage is an inferior condition for a Christian, and Hermas shows no signs of being embarrassed about the legitimate use of sexuality within marriage. And the ban on separated spouses contracting new marriages is related exclusively to considerations of forgiveness.[2]

The insistence that a fallen spouse can repent leads into a brief excursus on repentance, which is said to be an important form of understanding: the sinner understands that he has done wrong in the sight of the Lord and he 'repents and no longer does the evil thing he had been doing, but does good abundantly and humbles his own soul and torments it, because of his sin' (4.2, 30.2). Repentance involves an effective conversion to new behaviour, as well as a remorse which is evidently meant to be psychologically painful.

Then comes the passage we have already considered, about the teachers who deny the possibility of postbaptismal repentance (4.3, 31).

We then return to the topic of marriage, and Hermas asks whether it is sinful to remarry after the death of one's spouse, and he is told that it is not sinful, though remaining single will earn greater honour before the Lord (4.4, 32.1–2). The point is not elaborated, so we are not told why it is more glorious not to remarry. It looks as if Hermas was simply accepting the normal Christian belief of his time, without yielding an inch to anyone who might want to recommend a more rigorously ascetic policy. Hermas does not even show any signs of sharing St Paul's enthusiasm for a life of celibacy as being less distracted from concentration on the Lord.

The fifth Commandment is about avoiding bad temper and bitterness. This is not a problem for people who are 'full in the faith', but doubters are liable to get upset about all sorts of silly things, because their inadequate faith does not allow them to be free from care or to glorify God in all things, as full believers do. So they become bitter because of their foolishness, and this leads to irritation, which makes them lose their temper, and the final result is likely to be a settled condition of fury, which is 'a great sin and incurable' (5.2, 34.1–4).

Once again, it is not hard to see the connection that Hermas implies between the general virtue of 'simplicity' and the specific virtue of good temper. There is a connection at several levels. On the surface, bitterness and bad temper are incompatible with that 'decency which the Lord loves' (5.4, 34.8), and which is the product of inner integrity and simplicity. And at the root, it is the lack of a settled singleness and determination in believing which lays people open to the sort of upset which generates bad temper.

So far we have been looking at Hermas's moral teaching as if it were no more than a set of ethical instructions. But his ethics cannot be separated from his understanding of human motivation. In his view, we are motivated largely by powers whose ultimately origination is outside ourselves, for good or ill.

The crucial notion in Hermas's anthropology is 'spirit'. Whether 'spirit' is something with which all human beings are endowed is not clear. Since it can depart without terminating the life of the individual concerned (5.4, 34.6), it is certainly not to be identified with 'soul' or the vital principle of human life. It is probably best to regard it as something imparted to believers, presumably at their baptism. It is made to dwell in our flesh by God, but it is not simply *given* to us: it is a 'deposit' entrusted to us, which in due course we have to return to the Lord (3, 28.1–2). And he will not be pleased if we ruin it while it is in our keeping; he gave it to us intact and expects us to return it to him intact, just as we expect the laundry to return our clothes intact (Sim. 9.32, 109.2–4). There is a close relationship between the indwelling of the Lord in the believer and the 'spirit' which God makes to dwell in our flesh, but the 'spirit' cannot simply be identified with the Holy Spirit. The 'spirit' received from God is 'without falsehood'; but people who do not love truth and become liars turn this spirit into something false, thereby 'cheating the Lord', because they do not give him back the 'deposit' they have received from him (3, 28.1–2).

There is, on the face of it, a slight inconsistency in the way Hermas talks about the 'spirit'. Sometimes he speaks as if the spirit itself becomes corrupted if we engage in sinful thoughts or behaviour, but sometimes he suggests rather that the spirit is unpleasantly affected by our sins precisely because it retains its own goodness. Thus it is a dreadful shock to an all-holy spirit, as we learned near the beginning of the book, if someone like Hermas conceives an unchaste thought (Vis. 1.2, 2.4). Similarly, in the matter of truthfulness, we are warned not to make the 'spirit of truth' cohabit with 'an evil conscience', which would 'cause grief to the decent, true spirit' (Mand. 3, 28.4).

There is a similar apparent confusion in the section on good temper, in which the idea of contaminating the spirit and the idea of distressing it are so closely interwoven that it is impossible to keep them apart.

> If you are good tempered, the holy spirit dwelling in you will be pure, not darkened by another, evil spirit; finding its accommodation spacious, it will exult and be happy, together with the vessel in which it dwells, and will worship God with great cheerfulness, being at peace in itself. But if any bitterness approaches, at once the holy spirit, being delicate, feels cramped, finding its place impure, and it seeks to leave the place, because it is suffocated by the evil spirit and has no place to worship the Lord as it wants to, being defiled by bitterness. The Lord dwells in patient good temper, but in bitterness it is the devil who dwells. So it is unprofitable and bad for the man in whom they dwell to have both spirits living in the same place. (5.1, 33.2–4)

Once again we notice the link between the presence of the 'holy spirit' and the indwelling of the Lord, with its counterpart on the other side, an indwelling of the devil associated with the presence of an evil spirit of bitterness.

Hermas is speaking much less figuratively than we might suppose. He believes quite straightforwardly that good and bad moral qualities derive from the presence of various kinds of spirit in us, and it is likely that he thought of these spirits (if he held any conscious view on the subject) in more or less Stoic terms, as having bodily existence of a particularly refined nature, which made them peculiarly capable both of permeating other bodies and of being mingled with other bodies, without losing their own identity.[3] The cohabitation, then, of a holy spirit with a spirit of bitterness really is like mixing wormwood with honey, which spoils the honey and ruins its sweetness (5.1, 33.5). A good spirit really can be contaminated. But, unlike honey, it is also characterized by a sort of consciousness and a certain freedom of initiative. There is, strictly, no contradiction involved in claiming that it can be both contaminated and distressed. And if it becomes too distressed, it will simply go away. That is why bitterness is such a dangerous quality in which to indulge. With its brood of bad temper, anger and settled fury, it quite crowds out the holy spirit:

> When all these spirits lodge in a single container, where the holy spirit is also living, the container does not have room for them all, it is too full. So the delicate spirit, being unaccustomed to dwell with an evil spirit and with hardness, goes away from such a person and seeks to live with meekness and quiet. Then, when it departs from that man in whom it was dwelling, he comes to be devoid of the righteous spirit and thereafter he is full of evil spirits and is unstable in all his activity, dragged hither and thither by evil spirits, and as far as any capacity for good thinking is concerned, he is completely blind. (5.2, 34.5–7)

It is *because* the holy spirit is driven out like this, with all that results from its departure, that the condition of the person who has settled down into a state of constant resentment is 'incurable' (5.2, 34.4–5).

Even if things do not come to this extreme, bitterness seriously hampers the working of the holy spirit. Good temper is sweeter than honey and is 'useful to the Lord'; bitterness is sour and useless and, if it is allowed to become mixed with good temper, it spoils the good temper, with the result that its 'prayer is no longer useful to God' (5.1, 33.6). And of course if prayer ceases to function, the Christian loses his most important source of help.

Since the presence and good functioning of a holy spirit, which is the means by which God dwells in the believer, is the foundation for and source of the whole Christian life, it is easy to see why Hermas insists so much on avoiding those qualities which, as it were, make life impossible for the holy spirit; and the foremost of these is bitterness. That is why Hermas's angelic mentor tells him that if he keeps the commandments about good temper, he will easily keep all the others (5.2, 34.8).[4]

The imparting of holy spirit to believers and the subsequent surrender and judgement of the imparted spirits is dramatized in the eighth Parable in terms of the handing over of willow branches, which are later returned and examined. When Hermas asks what the tree signifies, he is told that it is 'the law of God which is given into the whole world. And this law is the Son of God, who has been proclaimed to the ends of the earth' (Sim. 8.2, 69.2). In Hermas's rather confusing terminology (and it is only fair to remember that he was writing long before the language of Trinitarian orthodoxy was established), the Son of God is also called 'the Holy Spirit' (Sim. 5, 58.2; Sim. 9, 78.1). And the virtues called for by the law (which is the Son, the Spirit) are themselves both 'holy spirits' (depicted as virgins, perhaps under the influence of Semitic languages, in which the word for 'spirit' is feminine) (Sim. 9.13, 90.2; Sim. 9.15, 92) and 'powers of the Son of God' (Sim. 9.13, 90.2). Evidently the spirit given to believers can be seen as either single or multiple (just as the seven spirits in Rev 1:4 are not distinct from the Holy Spirit), in that it is certainly not to be distinguished from the spirits which are the virtues. It can be seen as one spirit, because the virtues (unlike the vices) form a coherent whole, just as the precepts add up to a single law (which is the Son of God). The imparting of the spirit is the same as the imparting of the law, and it is a real power that is given, not just a set of commandments. And it is this power which becomes contaminated, if evil spirits are allowed to come in too. This is why Hermas can talk about the sinner against truth not just making the spirit of truth into something false, but also 'defiling the commandment' (Mand. 3, 28.2).

In the sixth Commandment Hermas alludes to the scheme of the Two Ways, which we have met in the *Didache* and Barnabas. But whereas in the *Didache* (as in the letter of Clement) the essential gift of God is seen in the fact that he has shown us the way in which we ought to walk, in Hermas, even more explicitly than in Barnabas, we are dealing with powers for good and evil, not just with precepts. Hermas's mentor goes back to his first commandment, about faith, fear and self-control, and says he is now going to explain their 'powers'; and we are told that these powers are twofold, with regard to what is right and with regard to what is wrong. What is right must be trusted: it gives us a straight, smooth way. What is wrong must not be trusted: it gives us a crooked, rough, thorny way, full of obstacles (6.1, 35.2-3).

First of all, then, we are taught about the twofold power of faith, which is essentially a matter of knowing where to trust and where not to trust. And this is important, because 'there are two angels' with each of us, 'one of righteousness and one of wickedness'. The angel of righteousness is clearly closely associated with the holy spirit given to us by God, though the two should perhaps not be identified. Like the holy spirit, the angel of righteousness is 'delicate', and he is also said to be 'modest, meek and quiet' (6.2, 36.1–2). The angel of wickedness is characterized precisely by that bitterness we have been warned against, with its attendant foolishness. Not surprisingly, the two angels are associated respectively with all the works of virtue and all the motley array of vices (6.2, 36.3–5). But what is startling is that they both appear to have immense power over human beings. 'Take the most faithful man: if the thought of the evil angel arises in his heart, it is necessary for that man or woman to do some sin.' Conversely, if the works of the righteous angel arise in the heart of the most wicked man or woman, 'of necessity' he or she 'must do some good' (6.2, 36.7–8). This sounds like total fatalism, but that is clearly not what Hermas means. But the area of freedom left to us needs to be identified. What we can and must do is *trust* the righteous angel and his works (6.2, 36.3) and distance ourselves from the wicked angel and not trust him at all (6.2, 36.6). We must *believe* that the works of the wicked angel are bad (6.2, 36.10).

The point is brought out with some insistence in later parts of the *Shepherd* that the basis for effective Christian practice is a solid belief that what God commands is both good and practicable, in spite of all appearances to the contrary (cf. Mand. 12.3, 46.5; Sim. 6.1, 61.2). We cannot seriously become a prey to wicked angels or unclean spirits unless there is first a significant failure in faith. As we have already learned, it is those whose faith is insufficient who are vulnerable to bitterness (Mand. 5.2, 34.1). Probably the suggestion that even the most faithful man would have to do some sin if a wicked angel got hold of him is not meant to indicate a real possibility. Anyone who was really full of faith would leave no opening by which the wicked angel could gain access to him.

This is borne out by the seventh Commandment, which briefly indicates the twofold working of fear. We are to fear God, but we should not fear the devil, since he has no power over those who fear the Lord (7.1, 37.1–2). True, we should fear the works of the devil, but we do that precisely by fearing the Lord. So if we find ourselves wanting to do something evil, the remedy is to fear the Lord and then we shall restrain ourselves; and if we find ourselves wanting to do good, again we should fear the Lord and then we will do it, because the fear of the Lord is 'strong and great and glorious' (7.1, 37.3–4). That is to say, the real power is with the virtue; the devil is powerless, unless there is already something in us interfering with the power of the virtue.

The third virtue subsumed under the first Commandment was self-control. The Greek word, *enkrateia*, literally means 'keeping something under control'. In the eighth Commandment the twofold working of this virtue is explained. There are some areas in which control is good, others is which it is bad. We should control evil and refrain from doing it, we should not control good (8, 38.1–2). This is then spelled out in long lists of good and bad things that do or do not need controlling. The most interesting thing in this chapter is the general principle that we do good, not by exercising control, but precisely by *not* exercising control. The virtues and the commandments, in Hermas's scheme, give us a real impetus towards doing good, and this impetus needs to be given a free rein. This picks up and develops the moral lesson Hermas learned much earlier on from the Church, when she urged him to pray about righteousness as well as praying about his sins (Vis. 3.1, 9.6). Righteousness is a positive force for good and it should be indulged in. Hermas is willing to use the very hedonistic term *tryphē* in this connection, which would generally connote the sort of entertainments that moralists frown upon. 'There are delights (*tryphai*) which save people. Many people get a great kick out of doing good, and are carried along by their pleasure in it' (Sim. 6.5, 65.7). The holy spirit in us gives us, in principle, an appetite for good that should be trusted and indulged in without restraint.

The ninth and tenth Commandments take up the second and fifth, and develop the topics of unhesitating and undoubting faith (with no *dipsychia*) (Mand. 9, 39), and cheerfulness (Mand. 10, 40). The aspect of faith which interests Hermas here is chiefly prayer. Doubters do not have enough confidence in themselves or in what they are doing, so all their endeavours go wrong (9, 39.10), but people who are 'whole in their faith make all their petitions with confidence in the Lord and they receive what they pray for' (9, 39.6). Faith, as a virtue, has real power behind it, whereas its opposite has none: 'Faith is from on high, from the Lord, and it has great power; but doubt is an earthy spirit from the devil and has no power. So serve the one that has power' (9, 39.11–12).

Cheerfulness is important because misery is the 'sister of doubt and of bitterness' (10.1, 40.1), though Hermas concedes, apparently without much conviction, that there is a kind of distress which brings salvation. Misery is 'of all spirits the worst' and more than all others it 'corrupts people and drives out the holy spirit' (10.1, 40.2). 'And then it saves again', Hermas's mentor goes on, causing Hermas understandable perplexity, which in turn prompts the angel to give him a little lecture on the importance of probing the truth and studying divinity, instead of being content simply to believe (10.1, 40.3–6).

The essential thrust of the explanation that follows is clear enough. Misery is caused by indecisiveness and doubt, because people who cannot commit themselves whole-heartedly do not succeed in their undertakings and are then depressed by their failure. It is also caused by bitterness, when people get annoyed and soured about something. And in either case the resulting misery grieves the spirit so much that it denounces the offending people to God and departs from them, because it cannot stand misery or being cramped (10.2, 41.1–6).

This clear and simple doctrine is confused by the statement that misery 'drives out the holy spirit and then saves again', which is explained, in so far as it is explained, in connection with bitterness: bitterness attaches itself to someone and he gets soured and so 'again misery enters into the heart of the person who has been bitter and he is miserable over the deed he has done and he repents, because he has done evil. So this misery appears to contain salvation, because the person who has done evil repents' (10.2, 41.3–4). It is impossible to believe that any saving grief could really be caused by bitterness, which is by now well-known to us as one of the worst enemies of the holy spirit. And it is tempting to underline that this grief only 'appears' to contain salvation and to suggest that the repentance in question is only useless regret. Certainly Hermas is explicit that the misery caused by bitterness over something one has done causes grief to the spirit (10.2, 41.4), and his summing up of the Commandment is without nuance: 'So remove misery from yourself and do not oppress the holy spirit dwelling in you' (10.2, 41.5). On the other hand, he does seem to have committed himself to the proposition that misery both drives the spirit out and saves people (10.1, 40.2; 10.2, 41.1). It rather looks as if he is desperately trying to accommodate a doctrine he dared not repudiate (cf. 2 Cor 7:10), but could not actually make sense of.

All this talk of angels and spirits (which turn out to be a sort of fine matter with properties similar to liquids or gases) may strike us as quaintly archaic or annoyingly naïve. Archaic it may be, but naïve it is not. In Hermas, as in much of Hellenistic and post-biblical

Jewish moral philosophy, ethics merges imperceptibly into psychology. And Hermas is surely no less entitled to look for the source of human behaviour in elusive substances, which have their own reactions and initiatives, than modern popular psychology is to derive our conscious choices and attitudes from a mysterious entity called the 'subconscious', with its hidden reactions and purposes. If his spirits are alarmingly material, this does not make his system any more naïve than modern attempts to find a physiological explanation for mental phenomena. And Hermas's picture of human beings exercising their freedom and responsibility within the considerable constraints imposed by factors which they do not directly control, and which impinge powerfully within the motives and aspirations which drive them, is arguably both more realistic and more modern than the more extreme claims for human autonomy made by later church fathers in response to what was felt to be the unacceptable determinism of the Gnostics.

Hermas is certainly not guilty of the metaphysical solecism of regarding the indwelling of God in the soul in materialistic terms. He is explicit that God contains everything and is contained by nothing (Mand. 1, 26.1). His interpretation of the divine indwelling is essentially moral: God dwells in us in as much as he dwells in the virtues which we have by his gift. If these virtues are, in turn, identified with seemingly material spirits, this does not mean that God dwells materially within these spirits. He is their source and their giver, but they do not contain him any more than any other creature does.

Nor is Hermas's psychology naïve, though it is perhaps not terribly original. His doctrine of spirits requires him to view morality essentially in terms of psychological dynamics. He is, of course, far removed from the absolute psychological commandments which have bedevilled modern society, ruthlessly requiring us to be healthy and balanced and fulfilled (sexually and otherwise). The psychological morality Hermas inherited was forged by Judaism and taken over in some circles in the early church in response to a very particular question: what sort of character, what sort of attitudes are required, if we are to maintain our faith and our identity in the midst of an unbelieving and sometimes hostile society?

Hermas is well aware that self-confidence is a prime necessity (Mand. 9, 39.10): you cannot commit yourself solidly to believing in the God of Judaism or Christianity if you doubt your own ability to make a right decision and stick to it. And, in the context, an important aspect of belief in God must be the belief that whatever happens is governed by his loving providence, and is therefore to be accepted cheerfully. A spirit of bitterness and sullen resentment will continually undermine faith. Faith also needs to be nurtured by a strong allegiance to the community of believers, so the social virtues and attitudes which facilitate this need to be cultivated: a spirit of suspicion or meanness will soon lead to a breakdown of fellowship. And, granted that the demands of faith will sometimes seem impossible, we have to keep on coming back, with doggedness but also with intellectual seriousness, to the primary virtue of faith: God's commands are not and cannot be unrealistic. If we try hard to understand them, and resist the allurements of false promises of enlightenment, we shall discover them to be true and even easy. And if, all the same, the going is sometimes hard, we must remember that this is not yet the end of the story. Our hope is focused on what God has promised, not on what we can obtain immediately. This life is but a way, not a goal, and we must pick our way carefully, amid the conflicting pressures that we feel around us and within us, learning which to resist and which to succumb to. And if we are weak or perplexed, we must not hesitate to ask God for help. He is close to those who turn to him with all their hearts.

The temptation to seek more light elsewhere is, however, a real one. This is where false prophets come into their own, and the eleventh Commandment is accordingly devoted to true and false prophecy. As in the *Didache*, prophets are to be tested on the basis of their lives (11, 43.7), but Hermas also indicates a simple criterion by which the true can be distinguished from the false on the basis of their respective ways of operating. The false prophet identifies himself as 'bearing the Spirit' (11, 43.16) and positively attracts customers (from whom he expects payment) (11, 43.12). He functions just like a pagan oracle, answering people's questions, but otherwise having nothing to say (11, 43.2, 6). His services are strictly private, and if he finds himself in the assembly of the righteous, who are full of faith and are praying to God, he is struck dumb (11, 43.13–14). His clients are typically people full of doubts and dilemmas, staggering from one crisis to the next, needing 'authoritative' guidance about what they are to do (11, 43.2, 4). The false prophet reassures them with a mixture of truth and falsehood, but the spirit at work in him comes from the devil (11, 43.3) and is therefore earthy, powerless and foolish (11, 43.11), deserving of no confidence whatsoever (11, 43.17).

A true prophet, by contrast, never answers questions and never operates in private. In the Christian assembly, when prayer is made, the 'angel of the prophetic spirit' fills him and, being filled with the

Holy Spirit, he speaks 'as the Lord wills' (11, 43.9). The Spirit at work in him is from God and is therefore powerful and should be trusted (11, 43.17). He would be quite incapable of accepting any remuneration for his service (11, 43.12).

One of the moral qualities looked for in a true prophet is that he 'makes himself needier than anyone' (11, 43.8), which, at first sight, suggests an ascetic renunciation of possessions. But a very similar phrase occurs in a list of good things in connection with which nobody should practise self-control, and it is most unlikely that Hermas, who is elsewhere so indulgent towards rich Christians, is recommending voluntary poverty to everyone, and such an interpretation would make nonsense of some of the other good works contained in the same list, which can clearly be practised only by people with money (Mand. 8, 38.10). So what Hermas is calling for in the true prophet must be an attitude which it is proper for all Christians to adopt, one of radical humility and dependence.

One thing we learn incidentally from the eleventh and twelfth Commandments is that, just as it is possible to crowd out the good spirit, so it is possible to frighten off the bad spirit. If a false prophet comes to an assembly of good Christians, his earthy spirit 'runs away in fear' (11, 43.14). Similarly in the twelfth Commandment, which is about good and bad desire, we are told that, if any evil desire finds us armed with the fear of God and ready to fight, it will 'run far away . . . because it is afraid of your weapons' (12.2, 45.4).

The twelfth Commandment completes the teaching on self-control. We must shun evil desires, but there is a good desire, a desire for righteousness, which is inseparable from the fear of God, and we must let ourselves be entirely dominated by this desire, and it is to the strength of this desire that we should ascribe any victories we win over evil desires (12.2, 45.4–5).

The angel of repentance concludes this section of his teaching by bidding Hermas to 'walk in these commandments' and to exhort his hearers to do so, 'so that their repentance may be pure for the remaining days of their life'. In exercising this ministry given him by the angel, Hermas will achieve a lot, he is assured, because people will listen to him. Indeed, the angel himself will be with him and will 'constrain' people to listen to him (12.3, 46.2–3).

Hermas comments that they are beautiful commandments he has been given; but can they actually be kept by human beings? This draws from the angel the important teaching that 'if you tell yourself that they can be kept, you will easily keep them and they will not be hard. But if your heart has already conceived the thought that they cannot be kept by human beings, then you will not keep them' (12.3, 46.5). God created the whole world for the sake of human beings and subjected all things to them; can they not therefore also master God's commandments? Anyone who has the Lord in his heart can master them all. For them, there is nothing easier or more pleasant or more gentle than the commandments (12.4, 47.2–5).

The Parables present the reader with a series of images, designed to clarify imaginatively certain aspects of the Christian life.

First, Christians should remember that, in this world, they are living in a foreign land, in which it is foolish to settle down too thoroughly by acquiring too much property. Any day the ruler of the city is liable to oblige them either to abide by his laws or to leave. So what are they to do? Will they deny their own law in order to preserve their property? It is much better to make do with a reasonable sufficiency, and beyond that to accumulate the wealth that is proper to Christians by giving alms to the needy and by helping widows and orphans. That is the wealth which is devoid of anxiety and distress (Sim. 1, 50.1–11).

The second Parable uses the example of the elm tree, which is barren itself, but supports the fruitful vine, to illustrate the interdependence of rich and poor. The rich man is poor, so far as the Lord is concerned, but the poor man is 'rich in his prayer'. So the poor pray for the rich who support them in this world, and both co-operate in a good work, and the rich too win their salvation (2, 51.1–10).

The third Parable presents us with a wintry scenario, in which it is impossible to tell which trees are alive and which are dead. In the winter of this world it is impossible to differentiate between the righteous and the sinners among whom they live (3, 52.1–3). The fourth Parable shows us the same sort of scene in the summer: it is now clear which trees have borne fruit and which have remained 'dry and fruitless'. This summer is the age which is to come. It is only then that the difference becomes apparent between saints and sinners or pagans (4, 53.1–4).

The obvious moral is drawn, that we should strive to be fruitful. But the angel adds a rider: 'Keep clear of having too much business'. Having too many things to attend to in the world distracts people from their service of the Lord, so they become sinners. But confining oneself to a single line of business is compatible with serving the Lord (4, 53.5–8).

It is interesting how unascetic and unradical Hermas's Christianity is. Like the author of the *Letter to Diognetus* (Diogn. 5), he maintains that the outward life of the Christians is pretty well indistinguishable from that of their unbelieving neighbours. It is moderate involvement in the world that he commends, not complete dissociation. The rich have their proper place in Christian society. The image of the Christians as being foreigners in the land, which can easily be used to call for a radical separation from the world,[5] functions in Hermas only to dramatize the wisdom of not being too rich. Although the surviving sources for early Christian asceticism are mostly later in date than Hermas, it is almost certain that they reflect traditions going back to the beginning of the church, and it is more than likely that Hermas was aware of them. Just as, with gentle tact, he urges his message of repentance against the rigorists who insisted on a radical, once and for all, conversion, so he can surely be seen as urging his doctrine of moderate worldliness against the exponents of an ascetic religion demanding a complete break with all the social and economic structures of the world.

There is a similar, nuanced, plea against another form of radicalism in the fifth Parable, which is about fasting. There was, at least in some circles, a radical reinterpretation of fasting, which denied all value to literal abstention from food.[6] Hermas at first appears to go along with this, a tactic with which we are now becoming familiar. When he tells the angel that he is performing his customary fast, the angel says that people do not know how to fast, and then reinterprets fasting to mean abstaining from evil and keeping the commandments (5.1, 54.1-5). But, with the help of a not very illuminating parable, the angel goes on to introduce the idea of works of supererogation—works, that is, done voluntarily over and above what is actually commanded. And fasting, in its literal sense, can be brought back in as one such work, especially if the money saved by fasting is given to someone in need (5.1-3, 54-56).

The value of external works is then underscored on the basis of a doctrine of the incarnation, which is not totally clear, but which is evidently modelled on Hermas's understanding of how Christians are endowed with holy spirit. The incarnation of the Son of God is the supreme instance of this, and the complete fidelity of his flesh to the Spirit and its consequent reward establish for us too the principle that our flesh will receive its reward, if it is found undefiled. Conversely any defilement of the flesh entails a defilement of the spirit too—a doctrine Hermas claims never to have heard before (5.4-7, 57-60).

The remaining Parables are concerned chiefly with restating and defining what has already been said about repentance and the chances different categories of sinners have of repenting. The eighth Parable gives us another picture of the judgement, in which the image of the tower is re-introduced, and the ninth Parable (which is at least presented as having been added later [9.1, 78.1]) is an elaborate rerun of the vision of the building of the tower. The tenth Parable, which claims to have been added later still (10.1, 111.1), is a kind of epilogue, encouraging Hermas to persevere in his own Christian life and in his mission to the church. It will be most convenient to deal with these chapters thematically.

At the beginning of the ninth Parable Hermas's mentor draws attention to the fact that there has been a certain development in the revelations made to Hermas. At first he was capable only of seeing the Holy Spirit in the form of the Church; then he became strong enough to see angels, and then he came more immediately under the Spirit himself. But he has still got to receive a more precise and accurate revelation, and this is why the ninth Parable is added (9.1, 78.1-3). This alerts us to the possibility that there may be a genuine development of doctrine within Hermas's book, and that later parts may be intended to correct, as well as supplement, what has gone before. Earlier on, Hermas was more 'timid' than he is now, so he could not be shown everything precisely (9.1, 78.3). It is not unreasonable to take this as meaning that his doctrine at the end of the book is less timid than what went before.

One point on which there certainly seems to be a sheer contradiction is the doctrine of the second-class salvation for those who do not make it into the tower proper. In Vision 3 some of the rejected stones had at least the consolation of being left near the tower, and others were built into a second tower. In the eighth Parable there is no equivalent to the stones left lying near the tower, but there is the possibility of some stones being built into the walls round the tower rather than into the tower (the distinction is not made immediately clear in 8.2, 68.5, but it is explicit in 8.6, 72.6, and 8.7, 73.3, and 8.8, 74.3, the first passage suggesting further that there are several different walls, presumably at different distances from the tower). Whereas in Vision 3 it was quite clearly certain definite categories of sinner that were relegated to the second tower, even if they did repent, in the eighth Parable it is in most cases the speed or slowness of their repentance that determines whether people go to the tower or to the walls (8.7, 73.3; 8.8, 74.3); and the only class of sinners to which this does not apply is people who have corrupted the church with false doctrines which suggest that repentance is not needed—

and even some of them can make it all the way to the tower (8.6, 72.5–6). Presumably it depends on the earnestness of their repentance, if indeed it is not speed that makes the difference here too. In this second vision of the judgement, then, it looks as if no type of sinner that can be saved at all is excluded in principle from the fullness of salvation. In the third vision of judgement, in the ninth Parable, there is no hint of there being any second-class salvation anyway, and there is certainly no question of any unused stones being left to litter the ground near the tower (9.9, 86.5–6; 9.10, 87.2–3).

The elimination of the offer of a second-class salvation can be read either as a move in the direction of greater severity, excluding all hope from those who, under the earlier doctrine, might just have scraped through to some consolation prize, or as a move in the direction of greater optimism, allowing people who, under the previous doctrine, could only aspire to a second-rate beatitude, to hope that they might even get as far as fully-fledged beatitude.

The overall logic of Hermas's doctrine makes it probable that the second, more benign, interpretation is correct, and this option is confirmed by the sixth Parable. Here we are introduced to a rather fierce angel, the angel of punishment, whose role clearly corresponds to the punitive measures which finally and belatedly brought some sinners to their senses in the third Vision, enabling them to qualify for the second tower. The angel of punishment takes charge of people who have wandered away from God in their pursuit of the desires and deceptions of this life, without it ever crossing their minds that they have been sinners. When they have been sufficiently tormented by whatever worldly losses and pains the angel of punishment sees fit to inflict on them, they are handed over to the angel of repentance, who educates them well and makes them strong in the faith, so that thereafter they lead exemplary Christian lives (6.3, 63.2–6). These are clearly no longer envisaged as candidates for a mere second-class salvation. This is presumably why, in the eighth Parable, the possibility of a second-class salvation is now ascribed, not to any particular class of sinner, but to people who delay their repentance.

The final abandonment of the whole idea of second-class salvation can then be seen as going with a relaxation of the deadline which was said to limit the offer of repentance. Already in the eighth Parable the deadline seems less urgent. In this story the judgement consists in an examination of the willow-branches given to people from the tree, which is identified as the Son of God or the law. After the first examination the branches which were found unsatisfactory were planted, to see how many of them would revive (8.2, 68.6). Then there is a second examination, which reveals that many of these branches are indeed now quite acceptable (8.4–5, 70–71). But this is clearly not yet their last chance. In the moral explanation of the different kinds of flaw found in some of the branches, we are told that many of those who have not yet repented will still do so (e.g. 8.6, 72.6; 8.7, 73.2).

In the ninth Parable there does not appear to be any deadline except the completion of the tower (9.26, 103.6), which presumably means that we can forget the apparently arbitrary distinction made earlier between unbelievers, who could repent at any time up to the last day, and believers, who had to repent sooner (Vis. 2.2, 6.5), though Hermas still insists that his message of repentance only applies to people who have sinned in the past, not to people who propose to start sinning now (9.26, 103.6).

The earlier deadline for the repentance of fallen believers has not entirely disappeared from view in the ninth Parable, even though it is probably no longer being rigidly applied. People who have succumbed to wrong desires and been handed over to the 'bad girls' who are the equivalent, on the vicious side, of the lady virtues we first met in the third Vision, can still repent and be incorporated into the tower, we are told; but if they fail to repent, their place will be taken by someone else (9.14, 91.2). This is not overtly connected with any time limit, but it may well indicate why a time limit had previously been envisaged. The underlying idea is found in the New Testament too: because the people to whom God's invitation was first addressed failed to respond, the invitation is extended to others, to whom it had not been offered before (cf. Matt 22:2–10). It is in similar terms that St Paul tries to see a providential purpose in the Jews' failure to accept Christ, as making the gospel available to pagans (Rom 11:11). The point is made rather more bluntly in Acts 13:46. It survived into later theology in the form of a belief that the elect of the human race are intended as a replacement in heaven for the fallen angels.

It would certainly make sense of the limited jubilee which Hermas was originally commissioned to proclaim, if the lapsed Christians are given the first chance to repent, on the understanding that if they do not take it up, they lose the opportunity definitively, so that others can have a chance instead. It is quite possible that this was a line of reasoning current in some circles in Hermas's milieu; it is much less clear that it is how Hermas himself viewed the matter.

In at least one instance in the ninth Parable a reason is given why repentance must not be delayed until the last minute. The rich who have become too preoccupied with their business affairs and have tended to avoid Christian company, for fear of the demands that might be made on them, can repent, but they must do so quickly, so as to have time to 'do some good'. Only so will they win forgiveness for their past transgressions (9.20, 97.2–4).

Another relevant factor is mentioned in the seventh Parable. Hermas complains about his own subjection to the angel of punishment and is informed that it is for the good of his household, which can only be made to suffer if he, as head of the family, is made to suffer. When he protests that his family has already repented sincerely, the angel of repentance says that he knows this. 'But', he goes on, 'do you think that the sins of those who repent are remitted immediately? Far from it. The penitent must first torment his soul and be powerfully humbled in all his affairs and suffer all kinds of affliction; if he endures all the afflictions that are laid upon him, the creator of all things will certainly have compassion and grant healing' (7, 66.1–4).

Hermas's concern throughout is clear and consistent: he wants to assure everyone that repentance is possible, but without letting repentance be cheapened. It is a real conversion that is needed, and this implies both an inner rejuvenation and a change in outward behaviour. And he knows that this calls for an educational process in which affliction may have a significant role to play, and he is also aware that the crucial breakthrough for some people will lie in their discovering an ability to do good positively. His rubrics are at least susceptible of a pedagogical interpretation.

This brings us to one of the most vexed questions of all: is repentance objectively offered to all sinners, or are some sinners excluded even from the offer? When we read, in connection with a certain type of sinner, that 'for them there is no repentance' (9.19, 96.1), it certainly looks as if they are excluded in principle. And it is not difficult to identify the criterion by which some people are excluded. Two avowedly similar classes of sinner are introduced, yet one has the possibility of repentance and the other does not. When Hermas asks the reason for this distinction, he is told that the reason why one group can repent, even though their deeds are the same as those of the other group, is that 'they have not blasphemed their Lord nor have they been betrayers of the servants of God'. They will indeed be punished, but they can repent because they are not blasphemers or betrayers (9.19, 96.1–3).

If we examine the categories of sinners mentioned in the various judgement scenes, we do indeed find that in general nobody who has blasphemed repents. Many people who have denied the Lord in all kinds of ways do repent (8.8, 74.4), and even of people whose denial was totally sincere it is said only that the angel of repentance 'does not know if they can live' (9.26, 103.5). But of those who have combined denial with blasphemy not a single one repents (8.8, 74.2). Blasphemers and betrayers of the church are totally dead to God and none of them repents (8.6, 72.4). There is no life-giving repentance for those who have been frolicking in vain delights and in addition have blasphemed the Lord's name (6.2, 62.3).

Before we conclude, though, that blasphemers are excluded in principle from the offer of repentance, we must notice that they have failed to repent even though the message of repentance was preached to them (8.6, 72.4). And Hermas's mission is explicitly directed towards everybody. *Anyone* who lives by the commandments publicized by Hermas will live (10.1, 114.1–2). This suggests that no one is excluded *a priori*; it is simply the case that some classes of sinners do not repent, though they could have done so in principle.

Hermas seems to be hovering slightly uncomfortably between an objective and a subjective interpretation of why blasphemers are, at least in effect, excluded from repentance. The crowning horror of their condition is that they have been 'ashamed of the name of the Lord which was invoked upon them' (8.6, 72.4), which echoes the principle formulated in the gospel that the Lord will be embarrassed to acknowledge before the Father those who have been embarrassed to acknowledge him on earth (Luke 9:26). But it is also surely open to a more psychological interpretation. There can be no doubt about Hermas's awareness of the psychological factors involved in repentance; witness his distinction between those who have denied 'from the heart' and those who have not, and between those who have indulged in long-term and persistent divisive behaviour and those who have not (9.26, 103.5; 9.23, 100.3). And in each case the seriousness of the person's subjective involvement in his fault is said to increase the *difficulty* there is in his being restored to life (ibid.). It is at least possible that the blasphemers are regarded as beyond hope because they have put themselves in a position where they are simply incapable any longer of hearing the message of Christian hope. Their repudiation of the gospel goes beyond that of people who have merely yielded to temptation and denied their faith, because they have actually come to dislike Christianity, and any remedial measures which might be taken would only increase their dislike.

Whatever the proper interpretation of the fate of blasphemers, it is clear that on the whole it is subjective factors which decide to what extent different kinds of sinner heed the message of repentance. And the detailed exploration of the different kinds of sinner reinforces the psychological ethics expounded in the Commandments. What is essentially at issue throughout is the psychological conditions required for fidelity or for a return to fidelity to the gospel.

In the last analysis, though, it is perhaps not necessary to choose between a subjective and an objective interpretation. Although the doctrine of grace had not yet been subjected to the rigorous and agonized scrutiny which it received from St Augustine, one of the basic problems has already arisen for Hermas. He asks why not everyone repents, and he is answered, 'The Lord has given repentance to those whose hearts he saw would become pure, who would serve him whole-heartedly. But he has not given repentance to those whose crookedness and wickedness he saw, who he saw would repent hypocritically, in case they should again blaspheme his law' (8.6, 72.3). It is not a solution that would appeal to Augustine, but it does attempt to draw together the divine initiative, giving repentance objectively to some and not to others, and the subjective factors involved in repentance.

In the course of the ninth Parable, the lady virtues we met in the third Vision make a dramatic reappearance, together with their counterpart, the wild girls, on the side of vice. This time there are twelve of them, whose names are duly given in a list of virtues (9.15, 92.2). They are the guardians of the tower, while it is being built (9.5, 82.1). So, when the angel proposes to go away for a while, Hermas, to his utter confusion, is left to spend the night alone with the twelve virgins, who are clearly in a jolly mood. They insist that he is to sleep with them 'like a brother, not a husband'. Disregarding his embarrassment, the senior virgin begins to kiss him and hug him, and the others then follow suit and start a tremendous romp. Hermas begins to feel younger and joins in the fun, which turns into quite a dance. When it is done, he is obliged to go to bed right in the middle of all twelve ladies—he spent the night praying, he tells us! In the morning the angel returns and asks the girls whether they have been behaving themselves properly, and they tell him to ask Hermas. Hermas assures him that he had a lovely time (9.10–11, 87.5–88.8).

Commentators have been duly surprised at this episode, wondering how the 'austere' Hermas can permit himself such an outbreak of erotic mischief. It has sometimes been surmised that he may be offering a justification for the practice of *virgines subintroductae* (men and women living together in the utmost intimacy, but without any breach of celibacy).[7]

At least part of the alleged difficulty is unreal. Hermas's morality is anything but 'austere'. If we have been paying attention to the Commandments, we have already learned that virtue is a matter of yielding to the right kind of desire, even the right kind of self-indulgence. We have already learned that repentance rejuvenates the spirit. The charming and humorous picture Hermas gives us of his night with the virgin virtues shows us what it is like to become young again and to enjoy the life of the spirit. It is not whole-hearted Christianity that is grim and earnest, it is rather the attitude of the ditherers, torn between belief and disbelief, between worldliness and religion. Worldly delights are feeble and deceptive, and worriers constantly miss the real point of life. The only people who really know how to enjoy themselves are the true believers who cast their cares upon the Lord and become innocent and young in their fullness of faith.

Whether or not the practice of celibate intimacy between the sexes already existed in the time of Hermas is uncertain,[8] but the theory underlying the practice almost certainly did,[9] and without it, it is hard to see how Hermas could have written his story the way he did. It is at least possible that we should see him as, once again, reacting to Christian radicalism sympathetically, but with some serious reservations. The recovery of innocence should indeed result in a new freedom from inhibitions and in a new frankness between the sexes; but Hermas will not allow that any encratite conclusions follow from this. Rather than calling for a new, and somewhat preposterous, Christian ascetic practice, the dream of recovered sexual innocence is best left to provide a charming allegory with which to cheer the everyday attempt which all Christians must make to practise the virtues and to live with their fellow Christians (including Mrs Hermas).

Notes

1   *2 Clement* 12.2; Clement of Alexandria, *Strom.* III, 92–93, identifies the source as the Gospel of the Egyptians.
2   This makes it likely that, when Hermas was told that his wife would become his 'sister' (Vis. 2.2, 6.3), this means that she will become

someone with whom he can live in true Christian companionship, but not that they will thereafter live together as celibates.

3   On the materialism of Stoic physics, cf. A. A. Long, *Hellenistic Philosophy* (London, 1974), pp. 152–60; on spirit and its capacity to 'mix', cf. A. A. Long and D. N. Sedley, *The Hellenistic Philosophers* I (Cambridge, 1987), pp. 272–94. It is worth recalling that Tertullian, who was no mean philosopher, argued for the bodily nature of the human soul (*De Anima* 5), and that Origen and Evagrius maintained that angels and demons have bodies (Jerome, *Contra Ioannem Hier.* 16; Evagrius, *Keph. Gnos.* II, 68, 76, 82). The bodily nature of angels is also affirmed by Pseudo-Macarius (*Hom.* 4.9) and by Cassian (*Conf.* 7.13). Even John Damascene is unwilling to say more than that angels are unbodily by comparison with our material bodies (*Fid. Orthod.* 26; *De Imaginibus* 3.25).

4   Strictly he says 'the other commandments which I am going to give you', but in fact the remaining commandments are largely a review of those already given, so we may take the angel as meaning that the avoidance of bitterness will facilitate the keeping of all the commandments.

5   Imagery similar to that of Hermas is used in a much more radical context in the Gospel of Thomas (logion 21); cf. also Acts of Thomas 61, and other material discussed in G. Quispel, 'L'Evangile selon Thomas et les origines de l'ascèse chrétienne' in *Aspects du Judéo-Christianisme* (Paris, 1965), especially pp. 42–4.

6   It looks as if this may be the position of Barnabas (3.1–5), and it is certainly the position of the Gospel of Thomas (logion 14).

7   For both points, cf. the notes by J. Roly in his Sources Chrétiennes edition (Paris, 1968), pp. 312–15).

8   It is possibly alluded to in 1 Cor 7:38, but most commentators do not favour this interpretation.

9   It is difficult to believe that the development of the sequence of episodes in Matthew 19 is not intended to suggest a connection between celibacy, becoming like a child and the renunciation of property, and it is precisely this grouping of ideas which underlies encratism and celibate cohabitation. The recovery of sexual innocence and the consequent possibility of a new relationship between the sexes is clearly part of the meaning of the saying in the Gospel of the Egyptians about the two becoming one (cf. above, note 1), and the whole idea seems to be deeply rooted in Jewish speculation about the Messiah slaying the 'evil impulse', which is what sustains the drive towards both marriage and business. Cf. the note on the 'evil impulse' in W. D. Davies, *Paul and Rabbinic Judaism* (London, 1970), pp. 21–7.

5

Clement of Rome

The 'first letter of Clement' presents itself as a letter from 'the church of God sojourning in Rome to the church of God sojourning in Corinth'. No specific author is mentioned, but the ascription to Clement is regularly attested from soon after the middle of the second century and is generally accepted. Irenaeus, probably following a Roman tradition culled during his visit to Rome in about 175, identifies Clement as the third Bishop of Rome, after Peter and Linus.[1]

Although the letter was addressed to a particular church in particular circumstances, it was treasured in Corinth, where it was still being read publicly during the Sunday liturgy under Bishop Dionysius (c. 170),[2] and it was quickly disseminated to other churches. Eusebius reports that it was being used in a great many churches in his own time.[3]

The letter to the Corinthians is called the 'first letter' because subsequently another 'letter' was ascribed to Clement, not to mention a variety of other documents, which were recognized even in antiquity as not belonging to the same author at all.[4]

The genuine letter was written in response to a schism that was tearing the Corinthian church apart. In the absence of other information, we must glean from Clement himself whatever light we can about the nature of the problem and the significance of the Roman response, and this is not made easier by his courteous preference for formulating most of his points in quite general terms ('Let us accept being disciplined' [56.2] and so on), so that often we cannot be sure how far he is aiming his remarks specifically at the people he

89

regarded as the offenders in Corinth. Although he does sometimes address them directly, most of the time he contents himself with exhortations which could in principle apply to all Christians everywhere. No doubt this is one reason why the letter was considered valuable in circumstances quite other than those which prompted its writing.

The letter has generally been dated c. 95–96, but a good case can be made for an earlier date (69–70).[5]

Although Clement refers to the mutual admonition and correction which Christians ought to offer to and accept from each other (56.2), there is no mistaking the authoritative tone in which he calls the originators of the Corinthian troubles to repentance (57.1–2). He is conscious of speaking to them in God's name and he warns them that disobedience towards what he is saying would have dangerous consequences for them (59.1). Whatever the outcome, however, the Roman church will have done its duty in attempting to restore peace in Corinth, so 'we shall be blameless of this sin' (59.2). If the recalcitrant Corinthians obey the Roman appeal, 'you will cause us joy and exultation' (63.2). Clement describes his letter as, precisely, an 'appeal', but that it is meant to have a quasi-legal force is suggested by his remark that the Roman church is sending to Corinth men 'who have lived blamelessly among us from their youth up to old age' who will be 'witnesses between you and us' (63.3).

Clement's apology, at the beginning of the letter, for being so slow to attend to the Corinthian controversy (1.1) suggests that the Roman church may be responding to some kind of request from Corinth, but, whether or not its intervention was solicited, the Roman church, through its spokesman Clement, seems confident that it has the authority to intervene. It would be anachronistic to interpret this authority in terms of any developed notion of the primacy of the Roman church, let alone the primacy of the Pope, since it is probably only with hindsight that Clement can be called 'Pope', but it does look as if the Roman church was already conscious of having, and was accepted as having, some sort of responsibility for the well-being of churches other than its own local congregation.

The troubles in Corinth were plainly grave enough and well enough known to have caused considerable distress to believers and some scandal to unbelievers. 'Your schism has corrupted many people, has thrown many into discouragement and many into a state of uncertainty and it has made everyone unhappy' (46.9). 'This report has not only reached us, it has also reached people of a different persuasion from our own, so that the Lord's name is blasphemed because of your folly' (47.7).

One of the plainest statements of what is going on in Corinth comes in 47, where Clement compares the present situation with the one St Paul had to deal with. Then too the Corinthian church was afflicted with a divisive spirit of partisanship, but at least the people to whom different factions were giving their excessive allegiance were properly attested apostles or, in the case of Apollos, someone vouched for by the apostles. Now the position is even worse. 'It is shameful, beloved, it is very shameful, it is unworthy of Christian conduct, that the solid and ancient church of Corinth should be reported to be in revolt against its presbyters for the sake of one or two personalities' (47.6). Some irreproachable presbyters, after long service, have evidently been ousted from their ministry in a way which Clement considers unjust and sinful (44.3–6).

As was normal in the Pauline churches, the church in Corinth had a régime of *episkopoi* and deacons. It is clear from Clement that there is as yet no distinction between *episkopoi* and presbyters (44.4–5). Clement puts forward two arguments to show the necessity of this hierarchical polity, both of them destined to become important elements in Christian self-understanding. First of all, he appeals to the Old Testament to show that the principle of hierarchy, especially in connection with divine worship, was established and willed by God. There is a specific role allotted to the high priest, to priests, to Levites and to the laity.[6] No one is allowed to trespass beyond the appointed bounds laid down for his rank (40.1–41.1). When some of the Israelites challenged the established order, Aaron's right to his position was proved by a miracle (43).

Secondly, Clement argues that the apostles established a similar hierarchy in the Christian church. Christ was sent by God, the apostles were sent by Christ and they in turn appointed *episkopoi* and deacons in the places they evangelized (42). And they arranged for an orderly succession to continue thereafter precisely because they foresaw that there would be quarrels over church leadership (44.1–2).

The hierarchy of the church, then, is validated by the authority of Scripture and by the principle of apostolic succession, which itself derives its authority ultimately from God. Any attempt to dislodge properly-appointed presbyters, who have not been guilty of any misconduct, is therefore an act of sedition.

What motivated the 'rebellion' we have to surmise from Clement's reaction to it. Since he harps on the theme of jealousy, he must have supposed that this was a significant factor in the situation. But he implies that the 'rebels' were not simply out to get power for its own sake. 'You are[7] quarrelsome, brethren, and jealous over the means of salvation' (45.1). The dispute in Corinth about who should lead the church was essentially a dispute about the nature and 'mechanics' of salvation. In some ways the problem was caused by the very success and strength of the Corinthian church (3). Clement repeatedly refers to their profound knowledge of Scripture, but increased knowledge means increased risk (41.4). It looks as if some people were using their expertise to challenge the authority of the established clergy, and so Clement had to find ways of discrediting such people.

The basic objection to them is that they are pushing themselves forward, and 'God hates self-praisers' (30.6). Christ could have presented himself magnificently in a style befitting his status, but he did not do so; he came in humility, the despised Servant of the Lord (16). And the same pattern is found over and over again: those who are attested as God's friends and saints were always humble (17-18). And this is what God himself commanded: 'The wise should not boast of their wisdom, nor the strong of their strength nor the rich of their wealth; anyone who boasts should boast in the Lord' (13.1). Therefore 'it is just and holy that we should be obedient to God rather than follow the instigators of hateful jealousy in their boasting and unruliness' (14.1). Following them is simply surrendering to merely human wishes, and doing that is courting danger and disaster (14.2). The rebels may be able to make a very good case for themselves, but they are really devoid of genuine Christian understanding. 'It is right for us not to be deserters from God's will. It is much better to fall foul of foolish men, who lack understanding and set themselves up and boast in the magnificence of their words, than to fall foul of God' (21.4-5).

The very fact that the rebels have ousted unobjectionable men from their ministry shows them up as enemies of God. 'You have pored over the sacred Scriptures. . . . You will not find that righteous people have been thrown out by anyone holy. The righteous were persecuted, but by sinners. . . . Was it by Godfearing men that Daniel was cast into the lions' den?' (45.2-5).

As in the time of St Paul, the problem in Corinth was that too many people were too gifted. There is nothing in Clement's letter to suggest that in his time the Corinthians were still unduly interested in what we now, rather pleonastically, call 'charismatic gifts', but it looks as if there were people who thought that their understanding of the gospel and their spiritual prowess gave them a better claim to lead the church and to preside at its liturgy than the official clergy had. Clement therefore has to repeat Paul's message, using the same analogy of the human body:

> The great cannot exist without the small, nor the small without the great. There is a mixture in all things, and all this serves a useful purpose. Take our own body: the head is nothing without the feet, and the feet are similarly nothing without the head. The least members of our body are necessary and useful to the body as a whole. They all conspire together and practise a common submission so that the whole body is saved. So let our whole body in Christ Jesus be saved. Let each individual be subject to his neighbour, according to the position he is placed in by the gift he has from God. (37.4–38.1)

Strong and weak, rich and poor should behave to each other in the appropriate way, and the wise should show their wisdom, not in words, but in good deeds. The humble should leave it to others to appreciate them. The chaste should not boast, knowing that their continence is given them 'by another' (38.2). We should all reflect on the material from which we were created and from 'what a tomb and darkness' we were brought into this world by our Creator. His kindness to us started before we were even born. It is from him that we have all that we have, so we owe it to him to be grateful for everything (38.3–4).

People may mock us,[8] preferring a more self-assertive stance; but in reality what can a mortal do, what strength is there in anyone born of the earth? (39.2). With the help of a long quotation from Job, Clement shows that no one stands the slightest chance of either resisting God or justifying himself in God's sight. Even the angels, even heaven itself is not pure in God's sight (39.3–9). The only possible conclusion from these 'obvious' reflections is that we ought to do everything in an orderly way in accordance with God's commandments (40.1). Clement then launches into his proof of the divine authority which underlies the church's hierarchy.

As Clement sees it, the disarray in the Corinthian church needs to be remedied by a revival of faith (27.3). The trouble with the rebels is that they have too much confidence in their own resources. We are God's chosen people (29), and our commendation must come from him, not from ourselves (30). 'Self-assertiveness, stubbornness, temerity, these things belong to those who are cursed by God; a yielding, humble, meek attitude is what is found among those who have been blessed by God' (30.8). We should cleave to God's blessing, and so we need to examine what the 'ways of his blessing' are (31.1). And what we find is that Abraham was blessed because he performed righteousness 'through faith', and that Isaac offered himself in sacrifice because of his confidence in God and his knowledge of what was to come, and that Jacob humbly yielded before his brother and went into exile and served Laban (31.2–4). If we study the evidence carefully, we shall recognize the greatness of God's gifts. From him come priests and Levites, from him comes the incarnate Lord Jesus, from him come kings and rulers and leaders (32.1–2). And these were all 'glorified and made great, not by themselves or because of their works or their righteousness, but through God's will' (32.3). So we too, 'who have been called in Christ Jesus through his will, are not justified by ourselves or by our own wisdom or understanding or piety or by the works we have done in holiness of heart, but by faith' (32.4).

If we are justified by faith, does this mean that we should refrain from doing good and abandon charity? Certainly not! The Lord himself exults in his works, and all the righteous too have been 'adorned with good works' (33). It is the good labourer who earns his bread, and it is similarly by exerting ourselves to do good that we put ourselves in the position of receiving a reward from God (34.1–3). Precisely because we believe in God's promises, then, we should strive to keep his commandments. God has already brought amazing gifts to our notice: 'Life in immortality, radiance in righteousness, truth in frank speech, faith in confidence, continence in holiness'. How much more wonderful, then, must be the gifts in store for those who persevere. 'So let us strive to be found among those who persevere, so that we may share in the promised gifts. And how is this to be done, beloved? By having our minds firm in faith with regard to God, by seeking out what is pleasing and acceptable to him, by putting into effect what is in accordance with his perfect will and by following the way of truth . . .' (35.1–5).

Far from there being any conflict between faith and works, it is precisely faith, particularly faith in God's promises, that motivates works. If we want to receive the blessings promised by God, we must abide by the regulations he has laid down. The whole 'programme', so to speak, is 'validated' by faith in Christ (22.1).

Belief in God's promises is inseparable from belief in the visitation of God which is still to come, and the delay in this visitation must not be allowed to induce doubt or disbelief. 'The Lord will do everything when and as he wants' (27.5). Quoting an unknown 'scripture', perhaps a lost Jewish apocalypse, Clement says, 'The undecided, who doubt in their souls, are wretched. They say, "We heard all this in the time of our fathers too, and look, we have grown old and none of it has happened to us" ' (23.3). But, as the same 'scripture' goes on, the vine should teach us to be patient: there is a long process involved before we get to the ripe grape (23.4).

In particular we must not doubt the reality of the resurrection, of which God has made Christ the firstfruits by raising him from the dead (24.1). 'Resurrection' is built into nature, so Clement argues, so we should not find it surprising that the creator of all is going to bring about the resurrection of those who have served him in holiness, trusting in him 'with good faith'. Day and night are an example: when night 'sleeps', day rises again. Again, seed falls into the ground and breaks up, but from its breaking up 'the greatness of the Lord's providence raises it up again, and more grows from each one seed and produces fruit'. Finally Clement cites the evidence of the phoenix, which he obviously takes to be plain biological fact (24.1 – 26.1).

'In this hope', he concludes, 'our souls should be bound to him who is faithful in his promises and just in his judgements' (27.1).

It is tempting to surmise from Clement's insistence on the credibility of the resurrection that there were still people in Corinth, as there were in St Paul's time (1 Cor 15:12), who denied the doctrine. At any rate, hope in the resurrection is an important element in Clement's exposition of what Christianity is all about and why it is vital not to disrupt the appointed structure of the church. Living peaceably within the institutional church is an essential part of a life lived on the basis of God's ordinances, and it is worth living like this because of the hope that Christians have in an inconceivably splendid reward that God will give to those who remain faithful, when he comes to judge at the end of the world. And there are no other alternatives open to us, because 'what world will receive anyone who is a deserter from God?' (28.2).

However absurd it may seem to outsiders, people's position in the church depends simply on God's will. The rebels in Corinth were perhaps trying to turn the church into a meritocracy, in which their talents would receive due recognition. But the church rests, not on self-assertiveness, but on Christ, who has given us a model of voluntary self-humiliation (16.17). Both greatness and justification depend on God's will (32.3-4). 'Our boasting and our confidence should be in him. Let us be subject to his will', like the holy angels. 'Let us consider the whole crowd of his angels and how they attend upon his will in their service of him. Scripture says, "Ten thousands of ten thousands attended him and thousands of thousands performed their service of him and cried, 'Holy, holy, holy is the Lord of Hosts, the whole creation is full of his glory' ". We too, then, with one mind gathering together in a common accord, should cry out to him as with one voice, so that we may become sharers in his great and glorious promises' (34.5–8).

Although Clement does not develop any systematic Christology, he is in no doubt about the centrality of Christ. Firmness of faith and loyalty to the will of God are paramount because:

> This is the way in which we find our salvation, Jesus Christ, the high priest of our oblations, the champion and helper of our weakness. Through him we look up to the heights of heaven, through him we see reflected the perfect, exalted vision of God, through him the eyes of our heart have been opened, through him our stupid and darkened mind revives into the light, through him the Lord wanted us to taste immortal knowledge. (36.1–2)

Fidelity to Christ is thus the acid test of whether we are in line with or in opposition to God's will. It is Christ who gives us the provisions we need for our journey of faith, and with these we must be content. And that means being humble, not self-assertive, in subjection rather than in control, keeping Christ's passion before our eyes (2.1). This is the basis for the church's peace and for the 'full outpouring of the Holy Spirit' on everyone (2.2). Clement accordingly exhorts us to 'serve in God's army in accordance with his perfect commandments', with everyone obeying orders in his own rank (37.1–3).

The peace of the church is an objective in its own right (19.2), to be sought by imitating the humility and obedience of the saints (19.1). The whole creation is a great demonstration of peace and harmony in obedience to the will of God:

> The heavens, rotating at his dispensation, are subject to him in peace. Day and night accomplish the course appointed for them by him and do not hinder each other. The sun and moon and the choirs of stars unfold their appointed limits in harmony according to his decree, without any transgression. The earth conceives according to his will and brings forth at appropriate times abundant nourishment for human beings and beasts and all the creatures that dwell upon it, not hesitating or

changing anything of what he has prescribed. . . . The ocean, which is for human beings unlimited, and the worlds beyond it are regulated by the same rules of the Lord. The seasons of spring, summer, autumn and winter succeed each other in peace. . . . Even the smallest animals come together in harmony and peace. All these things the great creator and Lord of all commanded to exist in peace and harmony, giving his blessings to all things, but most particularly to us who have sought refuge in his mercy through our Lord Jesus Christ, to whom be glory and greatness for ever and ever. Amen. (20)

For the sake of the peace which there ought to be in the church any self-sacrifice is worth making, but this is because it is only within the peace of the church that any of us stands any chance of having our sins forgiven and of being brought to glory hereafter. Insisting on being prominent here and now, as the Corinthian rebels were doing, is shortsighted, because it cuts off the long-term prospect of receiving the blessings promised to those who abide by God's ordinances. 'Learn to be subordinate, dropping the self-assertive, proud stubbornness of your speech. It is better for you to be found within the flock of Christ, unimportant and properly enrolled, than to appear splendid and be cast out from hope in him' (57.2).

Clement's plea for the ending of the schism is a masterpiece of tact, combining firmness with sympathy. After deploring the scandal and distress it has caused, he says, 'So let us remove it quickly and fall down before the Lord and beseech him with tears to be merciful and be reconciled to us and to restore us to our noble and pure practice of brotherly love' (48.1). Brotherly love is 'the door of righteousness which stands open on to life'. There are many doors open to us, but the door of righteousness is this one, and it is in Christ (48.2–4). The other doors are evidently doors leading to personal greatness, but these are not doors to life, they are not doors in Christ.

Maybe you are faithful, maybe you are capable of expounding knowledge, maybe you are wise in interpreting what is said, maybe you are pure in your works. The greater anyone appears to be, the more he ought to be humble and seek the common benefit of all, not his own advantage. (48.5)

Notice that Clement does not exclude the possibility that the rebels may, in some sense, be better qualified in faith and understanding and virtue than the church's official leaders, but because of the contentious spirit evident in their approach to the means of salvation (cf. 45.1), they cannot be regarded as making a genuine contribution to the welfare of the church; true service must always be characterized by a humble acceptance of the existing hierarchical structures.

Clement then launches into a passionate celebration of the beauty of Christian charity, whose perfection is such that it defies all commentary (50.1).

> The height to which charity leads is beyond exposition. Charity fastens us to God, charity covers a multitude of sins, charity puts up with everything, is patient in everything. There is nothing mean in charity, nothing proud. Charity allows of no schism, it is not partisan, it does everything in mutual harmony. All God's elect have been made perfect in charity. Without charity nothing is pleasing to God. In charity the Lord took us to himself. Because of his charity towards us, Jesus Christ our Lord gave his blood for us in God's will, and his flesh for our flesh and his soul for our souls. (49.4–6)

No one is sufficient to 'be found in charity', except by God's gift, so we must pray 'to be found in charity, devoid of human partisanship' (50.2).

From Adam until now, every generation has passed away; but those who were made perfect in charity by the grace of God 'occupy the place of the pious, and they will be manifested at the time of the visitation of Christ's kingdom'. It was the common belief in the early church that, after death, a special place was reserved for the righteous, where they waited for the last judgement and the resurrection. Clement specifies that the qualification for admission to this 'place of the pious' is charity. 'Blessed are we, beloved, if we do what God commands us in the harmony of charity, so that through charity our sins will be forgiven' (50.5). Charity is therefore the essential basis for the hope of all Christians: because of charity our sins are forgiven, and because of charity the righteous are given their initial reward when they die. And there can be no doubt that the charity which Clement has in mind is fraternal charity, manifested in the peace and order of the church.

'So in whatever ways we have fallen, whatever we have done because of the enemy's plotting, let us ask for forgiveness. And the people who initiated the rebellion and the schism ought to look towards the hope we all have in common' (51.1). The Greek phrase literally means 'the common [thing] of hope', and it underlines the fact that Christian hope is common, not private. But within this common hope, there appears to be no limit to the possibility of sins being forgiven. The instigators of the schism are invited to repent in the context of all Christians hoping for forgiveness, within the charity of the Christian community.

> People who conduct their lives in fear and charity would rather fall victim themselves to all kinds of torment than see their neighbours hurt. They prefer to bear being condemned themselves rather than see the fine and virtuous tradition of harmony being condemned. It is better to confess your sins than to harden your heart. (51.2–3)

This moral is reinforced with hair-raising stories of what happened to people who rebelled against Moses ('They went down to Hades alive') and to Pharaoh and his troops who hardened their hearts (51.3–5).

If Clement's words are to be taken at their face value, the choice is a simple one, but not necessarily an easy one. If the rebels do not accept that they are at fault, the implication is that they are claiming that the inherited harmony of the church is at fault. They are not merely disrupting church order, they are *condemning* the harmonious situation that used to prevail. The issue raised is one which is familiar from many periods of Christian history, including our own: are people who disturb the peace with their reforming zeal to be condemned as agitators or welcomed as prophets who show up the peaceful church as complacent and compromised, whose challenge needs to be heard even if it does split the community and drive some people away?

Clement's answer is not as bland as we might think at first sight.

He begins with a general principle. The Lord of all needs nothing (this is a commonplace). All he wants is that we should confess—and Clement is perhaps exploiting the ambiguity of the word, which can mean either confessing sins or confessing God's greatness. In the context, however, it is the former sense which prevails. What God wants is the sacrifice of a contrite heart (52). This applies to everyone, so Clement rules out in advance any naïve view of the situation as being one in which some people are simply right and others simply wrong.

Then Clement reminds us of Moses. ('You know the Holy Scriptures well, beloved, and have pored over the words of God, so I am writing this to remind you.') While Moses was on the mountain, the people sinned, and God said to Moses, 'Let me destroy them and I will wipe out their name from beneath heaven and make you into a great and wonderful nation, much more so than this one'. But Moses would not hear of any such thing. 'Forgive this people their sin, or else wipe me too out of the book of the living.' As Clement says, this is an extraordinary manifestation of charity (54).

So, if there is anyone in Corinth who is noble and merciful and full of love, he should say, 'If it is because of me that there is rebellion and strife and schism, I will depart, I will go away wherever you like, and do what the populace directs. All I ask is that the flock of Christ should be at peace, with its appointed presbyters.' Anyone who does this will win great renown in Christ, and he will be welcomed anywhere. 'The earth and its fullness belong to the Lord' (54). No world will receive a deserter from God (28.2), but someone voluntarily going into exile for the sake of reconciliation in the church in Corinth is behaving as a genuine citizen of God's realm (54.4) and will be received anywhere in the world, since the whole world is God's territory.

Clement then cites pagan, Christian and Jewish examples of self-sacrifice. Many kings and rulers gave themselves up to death, in obedience to oracles, so that their citizens could be rescued from calamity. Many others left their cities, to prevent further dissensions. Many Christians have let themselves be imprisoned so that others would be released, or raised money to feed the poor by selling themselves into slavery. Women like Judith and Esther undertook appalling risks for the sake of the people of Israel (55).

The application of these fine examples to the situation in Corinth is left, no doubt deliberately, vague. They could certainly be taken by the rebels as a dignified way of stepping down. If the schism was started by people who felt a real concern for the church (and Clement never rules out this possibility), they could express that concern by imitating the generosity of Moses, who refused to let an unworthy people be blotted out in favour of a better people descended from himself. They could align themselves with rulers and leaders who sacrificed themselves for their people. And if they have to eat humble pie and offer to God the sacrifice of a contrite spirit, they can do so in the knowledge that that is what God requires of everyone.

On the other hand, there is equally a message for the official clergy and for the Christians who had not supported the schism. They too need a contrite spirit to offer to God. They too must intercede for the rebels, like Moses. And they too must ask themselves whether they are not in part responsible for the schism.

Clement certainly wants the long-established clergy to be restored to their position, and he is explicit that the leaders of the schism must repent and submit to the presbyters (57.1). But his mention of kings and rulers sacrificing themselves and their authority for the sake of their people cannot help but raise the question whether the unlawfully deposed presbyters ought not to consider voluntarily giving up their position and maybe even leaving Corinth. The important thing is not that any particular individuals should serve as presbyters, but that there should be a proper procedure for appointing the leaders in the church. The church exists as an objective embodiment of the divinely ordained way of salvation, in faith and hope; if its institutional structure were to be replaced by a meritocracy, in which leadership could be claimed on the basis of moral, intellectual or spiritual gifts, it would no longer have any relevance to the essential hope of the faithful.

Esther, whom Clement cited as the last of his examples of self-sacrifice, serves as a bridge leading into the next point that Clement wants to make. She is not only an instance of courageous self-exposure to danger for the sake of the people, she is also a model of self-humbling and intercession, and God 'saw the humility of her soul and rescued the people for whose sake she put herself in danger' (55.6). Similarly 'we should intercede for the people who are at fault in any way, so that they may be given the malleability and humility to surrender, not to us, but to God's will' (56.1). Neither side in the conflict is to triumph over the other; everyone is to pray that all those who are at fault will yield to God.

Then comes a quite general call to us all to accept being disciplined, at which, Clement says, 'no one ought to complain' (56.2). It is a very useful and good thing that Christians should admonish and correct one another, and it unites us to God, because he too 'disciplines those whom he loves', and being disciplined by the Lord is a great protection to us (56.2–16).

It is only now that Clement turns to address the initiators of the schism directly, calling them too to accept discipline and to subject themselves to the presbyters (57.1). 'It is better for you to be found within the flock of Christ, unimportant and properly enrolled, than to appear splendid and be cast out from hope in him' (57.2). It is those who obey God who have a reliable hope and whose appeals to God will be answered (57.3–7). It is people who keep his commandments who will be enrolled and numbered among those who are being saved through Jesus Christ (58.2).

Clement is not starry-eyed about the church. He knows that it takes charity, self-sacrifice and a humility modelled on that of Christ, to preserve peace and to maintain the proper hierarchical order in the Christian community. It may well sometimes be painful for gifted individuals to put up with the official leadership of the presbyters. But this is how God himself has appointed the way to salvation, and those who deliberately get out of step with it are automatically depriving themselves of hope. Rather than setting themselves up in opposition to the presbyters, such people should enter into the common enterprise of prayer and discipline, accepting criticism as well as administering it to others. It is not talent that justifies, it is faith, and abiding by the appointed structures in the church is the expression of that faith and of one's Christian hope to be saved, to be justified by faith.

The letter of Clement is an occasional piece, and we are free to wonder whether, in different circumstances, he would have expressed his Christian vision differently. But the general success of the letter indicates that his message was widely received as having a permanent and universal relevance. And it shows that, long before Augustine espoused a tolerant and comprehensive view of the church, against the puritanical exclusivism of the Donatists and the Pelagians, there was a recognized belief that individual spiritual prowess was less important than remaining humbly and peaceably in the institutional church, looking towards Christ in faith, hoping for salvation for oneself and for one's fellow Christians, praying for mercy upon all sinners, and putting up with everyone and everything in charity.

Notes

1   *Adv. Haer.* III, 3.3. In view of Clement's own lack of distinction between *episkopoi* and presbyters, we may wonder whether he was 'Pope' in the sense of being monarchical Bishop of Rome. If he was not, then it is not very profitable to argue, as some have done, that the letter must have been written before Clement became Pope. For a review of this and other arguments about the date of the letter, see the article by T. J. Herron, 'The most probable date of the First Epistle of Clement to the Corinthians', *Studia Patristica* XXI (Louvain, 1989). I am grateful to Father Herron for letting me see his paper.

2   Eusebius, *Hist. Eccl.* 4.23.

3   Ibid., 3.16.

4   Ibid., 3.38.

5   Cf. above, note 1. The case for an early date is argued, among others,

by J. A. T. Robinson, *Redating the New Testament* (London, 1976), pp. 327–34. However the fact still remains that the letter gives the impression of a church that has been in existence rather longer than an early date would allow for; and cf. Chapter 3, note 1, for further considerations militating in favour of the traditional date, *c.* 95–96.

6 This appears to be the first attested use of 'lay person' to mean some-one who is not a priest.

7 The Greek is ambiguous and could also be taken as imperative ('be', rather than 'you are'), but, granted Clement's strictures on rivalry and self-assertiveness, it seems more probable that it should be taken as indicative (as is done by Kirsopp Lake and Kleist in their translations).

8 'Us' here surely means 'us Christians', though it may be that Clement does also mean to show up the un-Christian attitude of those who set themselves up against 'us, the clergy'.

6

Ignatius of Antioch

The letters of St Ignatius of Antioch[1] give us an unusually intimate picture of the mind of a heroic and tragic churchman of the early second century. Arrested in circumstances we do not know, but which can be surmised, he was taken from Antioch to Rome (Eph. 21.2) to be executed, for the amusement of the populace, by being exposed to wild beasts in the arena (Rom. 4.1–2). In the eyes of the Roman authorities he was probably just another convict to boost the supply of victims for the macabre spectacles the Romans had come to expect, but in the eyes of the Christians his passage was no common occurrence. As word spread of his coming, the churches along his route sent delegations to meet him, headed by their respective bishops (Eph. 1, Mag. 2, Trall. 1), and he was evidently able to address the local Christians in the places he visited (Phld. 7.1). Taking the opportunity of a break in his journey at Smyrna, he wrote letters to the churches whose representatives he had met so far (Ephesus, Magnesia and Tralles); he also wrote a passionate appeal to the Roman church not to intervene to prevent his execution. If they let things run their course, he assures them, the martyrdom of 'the Bishop of Syria' in their midst will be the most important occurrence they are ever likely to be involved in (Rom. 2). Later on, from Troas, he wrote further letters, to the church in Smyrna and to its Bishop, Polycarp, and to the Philadelphians. Very soon afterwards these letters were collected by Polycarp, in response to demands for copies of them.[2] When Eusebius was writing his *History of the Church* at the beginning of the fourth century, the name of Ignatius was renowned almost everywhere.[3]

Eusebius places the martyrdom of Ignatius in the reign of Trajan (98–117), without being able to specify a more precise date.[4] Vague though this indication is, it is probably accurate. Eusebius also tells us that Ignatius was the second successor to St Peter as Bishop of Antioch,[5] information we may question more with regard to its meaning than its reliability. In what sense Peter was ever Bishop of Antioch it is impossible to say, and we may well wonder whether the shadowy Evodius was ever bishop in the strong, 'monarchical' sense advocated by Ignatius. It is at least quite likely that it was Ignatius himself who created a strong central church government in the greatest city of Roman Syria, and it is equally likely that he did so in the face of considerable opposition.

The church in Antioch was one of the oldest churches outside Jerusalem. The gospel was first preached there by refugees from the persecution in Jerusalem which had cost St Stephen his life, and, though at first they addressed themselves exclusively to the Jews— and Antioch possessed one of the largest Jewish communities of the diaspora[6]—it was in Antioch that some of them first began to preach also to the pagans, evidently with considerable success (Acts 11:19–21). If, as we are told, it was in Antioch that the followers of Christ were first called 'Christians' (Acts 11:26), it was no doubt because it was there that they first formed a significant body of people who were manifestly not Jews, and who therefore needed a separate name.

The church seems to have established itself quite strongly within a few years in the Syrian capital, seemingly under the leadership of prophets and teachers (Acts 13:1). For a time it provided a home base for St Paul (Acts 11:25–26, 14:26–27, 15:35). However, the combination in the same place of a strong Jewish community and an adventurous mission to the pagans made for a church it was hard to hold together. Soon there was a major controversy about whether or not, and to what extent, pagan converts should be obliged to keep the Jewish law (Gal 2:11–14; Acts 15:1–2). It rather seems that Paul's party, advocating a fairly radical separation between Judaism and Christianity, suffered quite a serious setback in the outcome.[7] It is certainly the case that a pronounced Jewish-Christian influence can be recognized in the church of Antioch well into the second century.[8]

Ignatius's episcopate must have represented a triumph for a more Pauline tendency in the church. His background and affinities are more Hellenistic than Jewish, and his views of church government are akin to those long established in the Gentile churches associated with the mission of St Paul, like those of Corinth and Asia Minor. He hardly ever refers to the Old Testament, but he is clearly well acquainted with several New Testament writings, though he probably did not yet regard them as Scripture. He shows himself unremittingly hostile to Judaizing Christians—and it looks as if he has in mind particularly Judaizing Christians of pagan extraction:

> If anyone expounds Judaism to you, do not listen to him. It is better to hear Christianity from someone circumcised than to hear Judaism from someone uncircumcised. (Phld. 6.1)

> It is absurd to talk Jesus Christ and to practise Judaism. After all, Judaism believed in Christianity, not Christianity in Judaism. (Mag. 10.3)

Ignatius was certainly heir to some Jewish-Christian traditions, but his own thinking was probably more indebted to contemporary Hellenistic religious concepts. His association of silence with God, for instance, reflects current 'theosophical' speculation,[9] and his exploration of the mystery of unity and the Oneness of God is somewhat reminiscent of Pythagoreanism and anticipates the development of Neoplatonist interest in the One.[10] On at least one point, as we shall see, Ignatius comes close to one of the Hermetic treatises. It is also possible that his famous phrase about there being within him 'a living, speaking water, saying, "Come here to the Father"' (Rom. 7.2), owes something to the Greek belief in water oracles,[11] of which there was one in the fashionable suburb of Antioch, Daphne.

It is probably this common religious background that explains the similarities that have been noticed between Ignatius's language and that of the Gnostics.[12] How far Gnosticism itself had developed in Antioch by the time of Ignatius is not clear. Menander, who is said to have taught in Antioch, perhaps represents a primitive kind of Gnosticism, though he appears from our meagre sources more in the light of a 'Christian' magician.[13] Saturnilus is a more convincing Gnostic, and he definitely taught a docetic Christology; but whether he was active in Antioch as early as Ignatius's episcopate is uncertain.[14]

It is from Ignatius's own letters that we have to glean whatever evidence we can about the situation in his church in his time. Although he was writing to churches other than his own and was in some cases aware of the problems they were facing, it is still reasonable to presume that the sensitivity he shows to certain particular issues was learned chiefly from his experience in Antioch.

As we have seen, he was worried about Judaizers. He was also worried about Docetists (people who denied the reality of the incarnation, maintaining that Christ only *seemed* to possess a human nature and body). More generally, he was worried about anything that would disrupt the unity of the church, which, for him, meant anything that was done apart from the authority of the bishop. He believed that there is no genuine church apart from the properly constituted hierarchy of bishop, presbyters and deacons (Trall. 3.1), and that without the bishop's authority there is no valid baptism or eucharist (Sm. 8.1–2). Granted such a view of the church, Ignatius's worries are just those that we should expect him to have had in Antioch. Even apart from controversies about Jewish observances and heretical views of Christ, which there is good reason to believe Ignatius would have encountered in Antioch, it is entirely credible that many Christians there, accustomed to the Jewish system of more or less autonomous synagogues within one and the same city, would have been out of sympathy with Ignatius's insistence on the single bishop as the sole focus of unity and authority in the whole territory.

It is clear from what Ignatius says that he left behind him in Antioch a church that was not, at least by his standards, flourishing.[15] In all the letters he sent from Smyrna he asked specially for prayers to be offered for his home church (Eph. 21.2, Mag. 14, Trall. 13.1, Rom. 9.1), and it looks as if it is precisely the absence of a bishop which is responsible for the situation that was making him uneasy: in Romans 9.1 he follows up his request for prayers with the comment that the church in Antioch 'is using God as its bishop instead of me; only Jesus Christ and your charity will keep an eye on it'.

By the time he wrote his second batch of letters, from Troas, good news had reached him. He now asks the churches to send delegations to Antioch to celebrate the happy outcome, as indeed the churches nearest to Antioch have already done (Phld. 10, Sm. 11, Pol. 7). The occasion for this rejoicing is that the church in Antioch is once again 'at peace', as he explains in each of the three letters. It has 'resumed its proper greatness and recovered its proper body' (Sm. 11.2). This language must mean that previously the church in Antioch was torn by internal dissensions and was, in some way, falling short of its proper greatness, that is, failing to live up to its proper standards and to retain the loyalty of its members. All in all, this must mean that Ignatius had been worried that the kind of episcopacy he had been trying to establish in Antioch would not survive his own passing. The good news can only have been that an acceptable bishop had, after all, been appointed to succeed him.

If this interpretation of the situation in Antioch is correct, as seems probable, it is only a short step further to suggest that Ignatius's arrest and execution were due, not to any pagan initiative against the Christians (for which there is no evidence in this period), but to the internal feuding of the Christians.[16] Pliny's policy, more or less endorsed by the emperor Trajan, was probably typical elsewhere in the empire too: if people were actually reported to the authorities as being Christians, they were liable to be punished and even executed, if they proved obstinate. But the authorities themselves did not actively pursue Christians.[17] The only other named martyr whose execution is dated to the reign of Trajan is Bishop Simeon of Jerusalem, and it is interesting that he is said to have been denounced by heretics.[18]

We may conjecture, then, that Ignatius was arrested because he had been reported to the Roman authorities by disaffected Christians. If this is true, his situation was indeed a poignant one, which might well account for some of the things he says about himself in his letters. When he remarks that he is not worthy to be called a member of the church of Antioch, he is perhaps echoing sadly the apparent verdict of the church whose bishop he was supposed to be. And it was, in a sense, a double failure for him to be thus thrown out of his own church. As a bishop, he saw himself as the linchpin of his church's unity, and he had manifestly failed to secure that unity; and he could not conceive of any true Christian life apart from the hierarchical communion of the church, and here he was, effectively unchurched. He was perhaps not just uttering polite compliments, when he expressed a hope to be associated with the church of the Ephesians in their eternal inheritance (Eph. 11.2). If the circumstances were as we surmise, it becomes rather less puzzling that he habitually refers to himself as if he were hardly yet beginning to be a Christian and as if his only real hope of salvation lay in completing his martyrdom. He had somehow to make sense of a particularly bitter personal disaster.

We shall return later to Ignatius's comments on himself. First we must consider more generally his account of what Christianity is all about.

Several of the themes we have already met elsewhere recur in Ignatius. Like the Didachist and Barnabas, he stresses the importance of Christians coming together frequently (Eph. 13.1, 20.2). Anyone who separates himself from the assembly of believers has automatically condemned himself by revealing himself to be proud, 'and God resists the proud' (Eph. 5.3). But, for Ignatius, both the nature and the purpose of this coming together of Christians are quite different from anything we have found in the *Didache* or in Barnabas.

In the first place, Ignatius wants Christians to come together, not to seek out the will of God, but to pray and worship, and in particular to celebrate the eucharist (Eph. 5.2-3, 20.2).[19] And secondly there is, for Ignatius, no question of Christians assembling legitimately without the presence, or at least the authority, of the bishop.

> Let no one be deceived. Anybody who is not within the sanctuary is deprived of the bread of God. For if the prayer of two people has such force, how much more does that of the bishop and the whole church? (Eph. 5.2)

Like Clement, Ignatius has a serious concern to safeguard the role of the lawful hierarchy and a confidence that we, as Christians, have received from God the knowledge that we need for salvation (cf. Eph. 17.2). But Ignatius's view, both of doctrine and of the hierarchy, is somewhat different from that of Clement. He seems to be uninterested in the procedures whereby legitimate clergy are produced; we hear nothing from him about apostolic succession. For him, what legitimizes the bishop, and therefore his clergy, is their relationship to the will of God in Christ, and it is this validation from on high that gives them their indispensable role in the transmission of the authentic life that is available for us in Christ:

> Jesus Christ, our inseparable life, is the will of the Father, just as the bishops, appointed even to the ends of the earth, are in the will of Jesus Christ. (Eph. 3.2)

And Christian doctrine is not so much taught as embodied in the structure of the church. The union of the faithful with their bishop and clergy is itself the 'offprint' (*typos*) and teaching of immortality (Mag. 6.2). It belongs in the context of a whole pattern of unities: rejoicing in his own brief encounter with their bishop, Ignatius writes to the Ephesians:

> How much more do I consider you blessed, who are united with him as the church is united to Jesus Christ and as Jesus Christ is united to the Father, so that everything may be harmonious in unity. (Eph. 5.1)

Ignatius admits that he is 'a man made for unity', so when he holds forth about unity he is doing only what we should expect of him. But he insists that he was acting under the inspiration of the Spirit when he cried out to the assembled Christians of Philadelphia:

Attend to the bishop and the presbyterate and the deacons. . . . Do nothing apart from the bishop, guard your flesh as the temple of God, love unity, shun divisions, be imitators of Jesus Christ as he is of the Father.

No one had briefed him to say this, even though, as it transpired, there was a danger of schism in the church there (Phld. 7.1–8.1).

'Nothing is better than unity', Ignatius writes to Polycarp (Pol. 1.2), just as he had told the Ephesians that 'nothing is better than peace' (Eph. 13.2), and the deep reason for this is that unity is what God promises and what God himself is (Trall. 11.2). Breaking the unity of the church or separating oneself from its hierarchy is a sin against the unity of God: offenders must 'repent and turn back to the unity of God and the bishop's council' (i.e. the bishop with his presbyters) (Phld. 8.1).

The structured church on earth is an image of the heavenly realities which give it its significance:

Be zealous to do everything in divine agreement, with the bishop presiding in the place of God and the presbyters in the place of the council of apostles and the deacons (who are most dear to me) entrusted with the ministry of Jesus Christ, who was with the Father before all ages and was manifested at the end. (Mag. 6.1)

The earthly bishop represents in the local church on earth the true and universal bishop, the Father of Jesus Christ (Mag. 3.1). And Ignatius seems to have at least a rudimentary awareness of the corollary of this, that each particular church, reflecting as it does a universal reality, must be in communion with all other churches, precisely because its true bishop, God, is at the same time the bishop of all the churches.

Wherever the bishop appears, there let the people be, just as wherever Jesus Christ is, there is the universal (catholic) church. (Sm. 8.2)

Ignatius is the first writer known to have used the phrase 'the catholic church', and his sense of the universality of the church is shown by his desire that all the churches should join with the church of

110

Antioch in celebrating its return to peace, and by his conviction that there is an immense significance in the Bishop of Syria being martyred in Rome.[20]

The interlocking web of unities is well brought out in the letter to the Magnesians, where Ignatius says that he hymns the churches, praying to find in them

> the union of the flesh and spirit of Jesus Christ, who is our entire life, and the union of faith and charity, than which nothing is better, and, most importantly of all, the union of Jesus and the Father. (Mag. 1.2)[21]

The union of Christ with the Father is the foundation of the whole system of unities:

> As the Lord did nothing without the Father, either in himself or through the apostles, because he was united, so too you should do nothing without the bishop and the presbyters. Do not try to make anything appear right privately, but only in common: one prayer, one supplication, one mind, one hope in love, in perfect joy, which is Jesus Christ, than whom nothing is better. All run together, as to one temple of God, to one sanctuary, to one Jesus Christ, who came forth from the one Father and is in the one and went to the one Father. (Mag. 7.1-2)

The union of Christ with the Father is the unity of God in his hiddenness and in his self-revelation:

> There is one God, who revealed himself through Jesus Christ his Son, who is his word coming forth from the silence. (Mag. 8.2)

It is his union with the Father that grounds the significance of Christ, and Ignatius is in no doubt whatsoever about the unique significance of Christ. Christ is the entirely sufficient revelation of God, so that, in face of people who refuse to believe anything they cannot find 'in the ancient records' (presumably meaning the Old Testament), Ignatius can simply say that, as far as he is concerned, the only relevant 'ancient records' are Christ himself (Phld. 8.2). The one thing that is special about Christianity is 'the presence of the Saviour, our Lord Jesus Christ, his passion and resurrection' (Phld. 9.2).

However, if the significance of Christ rests on his union with the Father, his relevance to us depends on the reality of his incarnation, which Ignatius tirelessly affirms against the Docetists. Just as we have seen Barnabas reinterpret the story of our creation in the light of Christ, so Ignatius insists that Christ is 'the new man' (Eph. 20.1), 'the perfect man' (Sm. 4.2), and it is as such that he is our life (Eph. 3.2 etc.). The reality of his human life is the source of our true life, so if we deny the integrity of his humanity, we automatically deny our own too.

> There is one physician, both in the flesh and in the spirit, begotten and unbegotten, God coming to be in flesh, true life in death, both from Mary and from God, first passible then impassible, Jesus Christ our Lord. (Eph. 7.2)

Apart from Christ, we have no true life. He is the bread of life, the bread of God, the remedy for death and the medicine of immortality, which is available only within the unity of the church (Eph. 5.2, 20.2; Rom. 7.3), and, since he is 'true life in death', we share in his life by 'volunteering to die in his passion' (Mag. 5.2), at least to the extent of humbling ourselves to accept the moral and institutional discipline of living within the church.

The combination of flesh and spirit in Christ establishes the continuity between his union with the Father and his union with us (Mag. 13.2, Sm. 3.3), and it is in both flesh and spirit that we must abide in him (Eph. 10.3). Ignatius has no truck with the radical separation between flesh and spirit which is the hallmark of Gnosticizing religion. He appears to yield the point, only to reinterpret it in an entirely orthodox fashion:

> Carnal people cannot do spiritual things, nor can spiritual people do carnal things, any more than faith can do the works of unbelief or unbelief do the works of faith; but even what you do in the flesh is spiritual, because you do everything in Jesus Christ. (Eph. 8.2)

To deny the genuineness of the incarnation, then, is to cut oneself off from the only true life which is on offer, and to make nonsense of the sufferings of the martyrs, including Ignatius himself. 'If, as some people say, who have no God, unbelievers, that is, he only appeared to suffer—when it is they who are only an appearance—then why am I in bondage, why do I pray to fight beasts? I am dying for nothing' (Trall. 10).

There is an extended anti-docetist plea in the letter to the Smyrnaeans, which is worth quoting in full:

I give glory to Jesus Christ, the God who has made you so wise. I perceived that you were fully established in unshakeable faith, as if you were nailed to the cross of the Lord Jesus Christ in flesh and in spirit, settled in love in the blood of Christ, quite convinced about our Lord, who was truly of the race of David according to the flesh, and Son of God according to the will and power of God, truly born from a virgin, baptized by John, so that all righteousness might be fulfilled by him; he was truly nailed for our sake in the flesh, under Pontius Pilate and Herod the Tetrarch. We are from the fruit of this, from his divine and blessed passion, which he underwent in order to raise up a standard for all ages through his resurrection, for the saints and those who believe in him, whether from among the Jews or from among the Gentiles, in one body of his church. He underwent all this for our sake, that we might be saved; and he suffered truly, just as he raised himself up again truly; it is not, as some unbelievers say, that his suffering was only in appearance: it is they who are only an appearance. Their fate will be in accordance with their opinions, since they are bodiless ghosts.

I know and believe that he exists in flesh after his resurrection, and, when he came to those who were with Peter, he said to them, 'Take hold of me, touch me and see that I am not a ghost without a body'. At once they touched him and believed, making contact with his flesh and with his spirit. Because of this they even despised death and were found to be above death. And after the resurrection he ate with them and drank with them, as a fleshly being, although in spirit he was united to the Father.

I make you this exhortation, beloved, knowing that this is the way you are in fact. But I want to warn you in advance against the human-shaped beasts, whom you ought not only not to receive, but, if possible, not even to meet. All you should do is pray for them, in case they too may repent, but this is difficult. But Jesus Christ, who is our true life, has power even in this. (Sm. 1.1–4.1)

In the letter to the Philadelphians, Ignatius makes a similar comment on Judaizers. After claiming that the prophets, the Old Testament saints, actually believed in Christ, he says that what matters for both circumcised and uncircumcised alike is that they should confess Jesus Christ. Otherwise, he says,

113

As far as I am concerned, they are only monuments and tombs of the dead, with nothing but the names of human beings written on them. (Phld. 5–6)

Belief in the human and divine integrity of Jesus Christ is intimately related to the unity of the church and the integrity of its life. People who deny the flesh of Christ must be written off as 'corpse-bearers' (Sm. 5.2), unlike true believers, who are 'God-bearers' (Eph. 9.2):

They have no concern for charity, for widows and orphans and the afflicted, they do not care about people being imprisoned or set free, or about anyone being hungry or thirsty. They keep away from the eucharist and from [the church's] prayer, because they do not confess that the eucharist is the flesh of our Saviour, Jesus Christ, which suffered for our sins and which the Father in his kindness raised up again. (Sm. 6.2–7.1)

It is the reality of the incarnation, of the flesh of Christ in his life, death and resurrection, that makes it incumbent on Christians to take their own bodies seriously and the bodily needs of others, and also to take the eucharist seriously and the body of the church. This is why, in a passage already cited, Ignatius combines the precept to maintain unity with the plea to 'keep your flesh as the temple of God' (Phld. 7.2).

This brings us to the third unity, which Ignatius wants to find in the churches: the unity of faith and charity.

Faith and charity play a vital role in the new, true life, which we have in Christ. Faith, Ignatius says, 'is the flesh of the Lord' and charity 'is the blood of Jesus Christ' (Trall. 8.1) or, as he says to the Ephesians, faith and charity 'are the beginning and the end of life: faith is the beginning and the end is charity, and the two coming together in unity are God, and all the rest that makes for good conduct follows from them' (Eph. 14.1). The new life has to be lived on the principle that, thanks to our union with Christ, God is dwelling in us (Eph. 15.3). Faith and charity together constitute, as it were, the divine presence in us, they are a real participation in the flesh and blood of Christ, and as such they have eucharistic as well as moral resonances and belong, as we should expect, inseparably in the context of the unity of the church.

It is difficult to quote Ignatius to illustrate particular points on their own, because for him all his main concerns are inextricably intertwined: true belief, structured unity in the church, moral qualities, not least those which maintain good relations in the church and with outsiders, such as humility and forbearance; all these things are part of what it means to live by faith and charity.

> I beseech you—indeed, it is not I, but the love of Jesus Christ—use only Christian food and keep away from alien plants, that is, heresy. There are those who mix up Jesus Christ with themselves, but with their honey-wine it is a deadly poison that they administer. Anyone who receives it in ignorant pleasure is taking his own death to himself in his evil enjoyment. So be careful of such people. And this will mean not being puffed up, being inseparable from Jesus Christ, God, and the bishop and the commandments of the apostles. He who is within the sanctuary is clean, but he who is outside the sanctuary is not clean; this means, anyone who does anything without the bishop and the presbyterate and the deacons is not clean in his conscience.
> It is not because I have heard of anything of the kind occurring among you that I write this, but to warn you in advance of the devil's assault which I foresee; for you are very dear to me. So take up meek forbearance and recreate yourselves in faith, which is the flesh of the Lord, and charity, which is the blood of Jesus Christ. Let none of you have anything against his neighbour. (Trall. 6.1 - 8.2)

Those who deny the reality of the passion are 'plants with a lethal fruit', they are 'not the Father's planting. If they were, they would show themselves to be branches of the cross, and their fruit would be imperishable, because in his passion he calls us his members' (Trall. 10 - 11). True faith, then, commits people to living in the light of the passion, and charity is the practical expression of this commitment, with both a sacramental and a social dimension. And the basic reality of living charitably and peaceably in the church, with whatever sharing in the passion this may entail, requires us to resist the allurement of high-sounding heresy. False Christians threaten the church both by oppressing its members and by seducing them with impressive talk. Either way it is necessary to respond with humility and gentleness:

> In face of their anger, you must be meek. In face of their boasting and big talk, you must be humble. In response to their insults, you must pray. In response to their error, you must be firm in the faith, being gentle in return for their

savagery, not striving to imitate them. Let us be found to be their brethren in our forbearance, striving to be imitators of the Lord. (Eph. 10.2–3)

Ignatius was well aware of the danger which he himself faced. As one who was suffering for the Lord, he claimed that he could scrutinize heavenly realities,[22] but it is not this that makes him a disciple of Christ, and he refuses to expatiate on such elevated matters, for fear of harming his hearers or readers (showing a reticence which was, no doubt, not imitated by some people who were much less well-qualified to speak than Ignatius was). He longs to suffer with Christ, but the very acclaim he receives as a confessor of the faith exposes him to the terrible risk of becoming conceited, so he has to remind himself that what matters is humility. He does not know if he is worthy to suffer martyrdom (Trall. 4 – 5).

Like Clement, Ignatius argues passionately in favour of remaining humbly within the proper order and discipline of the church, rather than flying off to the heights on one's own, but he sets this requirement in a much richer theological context than Clement does. He would, of course, agree with Clement that the ultimate reason why we have to stay in the church is that this is the way appointed by God for our salvation, and we must be content with the provisions he gives us for our journey. But, unlike Clement, Ignatius has at least the rudiments of a kind of metaphysics of salvation.

No one who makes profession of faith commits sin, no one who has got love hates. The tree is manifest from its fruit, and so those who profess to belong to Christ will be seen through what they do. Now it is not a matter of profession, but of being found at the end in the power of effective faith. It is better to be silent and to be, than to talk and not be. It is a good thing to teach, if the person who speaks also acts. There is one teacher who 'spoke, and it came to be' (Psalm 33:9): what he has done in silence is worthy of the Father. The one who has truly received the word of Jesus can also hear his silence, so that he can be perfect, so that he can act in what he says and be known in his silence. (Eph. 14.2–15.2)

This passage follows immediately after the declaration that faith and charity together, in unity, 'are God', and it is followed shortly afterwards by the plea, 'So let us do everything as having him dwelling in us, so that we may be his temple and he may be our God in us' (Eph. 14.1, 15.3).

It is tempting and probably correct to see a connection between what Ignatius says about silence and what he says about the divine indwelling. Christ, we remember, is the word coming forth from the silence, and Ignatius is probably aware of and presuming on a current tendency to associate silence with the divine. What Christ did in silence thus bears the evident hallmark of his union with the Father, and for us to hear his silence as well as his words indicates that we are understanding correctly the union of Godhead and manhood, of flesh and spirit, that there is in him. But the conjunction of word and silence has to be reproduced in us too, if we are to be perfect. If, in one sense, it is silence that guarantees reality, in another sense it is what we do that is the proper attestation of our genuineness. Talking needs to be validated both by its background in silence and by its insertion into the context of effective practice. And the tree is known by its fruit: what we do in silence expresses what we are in the inner silence of our genuine reality, without the distortion that can be brought in by words that do not come forth from any basis in silence. The model is God who 'spoke and it came into being', the God whose 'words are deeds' (Greek Enoch 14.22).

A mere profession of faith is of no value on its own. There are deceptive people who bear the name of Christian, while what they do is 'unworthy of God' (Eph. 7.1), just as there are people who profess to follow their bishop but in fact operate independently of him (Mag. 4.1). What matters is not that we should be called Christians, but that we should really *be* Christians (Mag. 4.1).

What makes us truly alive is a conjunction of inner and outer in us (cf. Rom. 3.1), modelled on and united with the union of flesh and spirit in Christ, who is himself inseparably united with the Father, with the ultimate mystery of silence, which gives substance to all that is truly real. If we try to live outside this pattern of unities, we are not the Father's planting, we lack the grounding in silence which is the condition for genuine reality, so we shall only appear to be human and alive, whereas in fact we are just tombstones bearing the name of human beings.

The unity of the church, on which Ignatius harps so much, is thus seen as an essential link in what we may call the chain of ontological validation. Christ is the one Jesus Christ who came from the one Father, without ceasing to be one with him, and he establishes in himself a unity of flesh and spirit, of inner and outer, and the unity of the church is the extension of this unity to us, who can only become one and coherent in our own individuality in as much as we accept and participate in the unity of the church. If at any point there is a break in the chain of unities, there will automatically also be a break in the process whereby ontological validity is transmitted through the mystery of Christ from the mystery of the Father.

The unity of the church, in Ignatius's view, depends on its hierarchical structure, which is an image of heaven. The bishop represents the Father, the presbyters represent the apostles and the deacons represent Christ. The bishop is the source of legitimacy for the whole church, and the church as a whole, living according to the commandments and to its own institutional structure, embodies Christian teaching. Ignatius seems uninterested in any teaching role the bishop might have; the only person he ever calls 'teacher' is Jesus Christ (Eph. 15.1, Mag. 9.1–2).

Even so, it is rather disconcerting to discover that a bishop with nothing to say receives a particular commendation from Ignatius:

> Let us strive to be subject to the bishop, so that we may be subject to God. And the more anyone sees the bishop being silent, the more respectful he should be towards him. (Eph. 5.3–6.1)

Widely divergent theories have been propounded about why the bishop should be revered all the more when he is silent. The simplest interpretation is that Ignatius is putting in a good word for the Bishop of Ephesus, 'whose quiet and modest demeanour might lead some to despise him'.[23] A silent bishop cannot compete with the impressive talkativeness of heretics or charismatically endowed leaders, but this is a reason for respecting him the more: they talk too much and their words lack substance; it is better to be silent and to be, than to talk and not be. By comparison with the dangerous doctrinal inventiveness of some people, the silence of the bishop allows the pure, apostolic teaching to be heard.[24]

Another possibility is that the silence of the bishop is a sign of his refusal to defend himself against the insults and injuries he may be exposed to. 'Like that Divine Shepherd whose under-shepherd he is, he must always be ready to lay down his life for the sheep and when he sees the wolf coming he must be strong and fearless in their defence, but helpless in his own.'[25]

Finally, there is the quite different suggestion, first made in 1950 by Henry Chadwick, that the silence of the bishop should be connected with the silence of God, whose image and representative the bishop is in the church.[26]

All three interpretations can be accepted, to some extent, as shedding light on Ignatius's meaning. In the immediate context of

Ephesians 6 it is unlikely that we are intended to jump directly to any thought of the divine silence, which has not yet been alluded to. The point at issue is that those who are too proud to submit to the bishop must realize that in respecting the bishop they would be respecting the God whose 'agent' he is. The bishop's silence seems to be mentioned as a reason that might be given for not taking him seriously. Ignatius's reply is, essentially, that, if the bishop is not impressive in his own right, that is all the more reason for respecting him as the emissary of God. The point is similar to one made in Magnesians 3:

> It is right for you not to take advantage of the youthfulness of the bishop, but to pay him all respect, in proportion to the power of God the Father. I know that the holy presbyters have not presumed on his youthful status, which can be seen by all, but, being wise in God, they submit to him—or not to him, but to the Father of Jesus Christ; for it is he, the Father, who is the bishop of all. So out of reverence for him who loved us, it is right for you to obey without hypocrisy; after all, it is not a matter of deceiving the visible bishop, but of cheating the invisible bishop. In such a case it is not flesh that we have to reckon with, but God, who knows all that is hidden.

Whatever apparent weakness there might be in the bishop's position, he represents the Father and, as such, should be obeyed and respected. No doubt silence could be seen as a disability by people who were looking for marvellous discourses on higher things or startlingly original doctrines, but Ignatius is suspicious of that kind of teaching, as we have seen. His preferences are revealed in his comment on the Bishop of Philadelphia:

> I was amazed at his forbearance. By being silent, he is more powerful than people who talk vainly. (Phld. 1.1)

If the silence of the bishop is, in the first place, only a sign that he is not endowed with eloquence or not inclined to compete with the verbosity of the dubious teachers who haunt the fringes of the church, it surely acquires nuances as we read further. The bishop derives his legitimacy from being 'in the will of Jesus Christ' (Eph. 3.2), the word coming forth from the silence, whose deeds done in silence were worthy of the Father. And his silence refers both to his hidden union with the Father and to his evident behaviour in this world. The bishop, like all Christians, must react to the hostility and boasting of false brethren with gentleness and charitable prayer, imitating the Lord rather than trying to beat them at their own game. And who was more wronged than the Lord, who more despised? (Eph. 10.2–3). It would be interesting to know whether or not Ignatius was familiar with the apocryphal Gospel of Peter, with its rather dramatic reference to the silence of Christ on the cross,[27] but it does not take an apocryphal gospel to alert us to the paradox of the silence of the word made flesh. Ignatius refers to three 'shouting mysteries wrought in the quietness of God': the virginity of Mary, her childbirth and the death of the Lord (Eph. 19.1). Although Ignatius's immediate point is that these three mysteries passed unnoticed by 'the ruler of this world', he surely appreciated the strangeness of the word coming forth from the silence only to be silenced in death. In Christ the silence of divine mystery and the silence of human defeat coalesce.

In his letter to Bishop Polycarp, Ignatius exhorts him:

> Be concerned for unity, than which nothing is better. Carry everyone, as the Lord has carried you. Put up with everything in charity, as indeed you do. (Pol. 1.2)

The bishop, as the focus of unity, has to be specially ready to imitate the Lord in bearing everyone and everything, at whatever cost to himself. The point might come for him, as it did for the Lord (and as it did for Ignatius), when no further response was possible except to endure in silence, even to endure being silenced. It is not in a mystic and glorious silence that the Father of our Lord Jesus Christ is most typically revealed, but in the silence of death, death on a cross.

How far Ignatius was conscious of these resonances when he penned his incidental reference to the bishop's silence it is impossible to say; but thoughts of this kind do seem to have occurred to him in connection with his own predicament.

Ignatius only once refers to himself as a bishop, and that is in connection with his impending martyrdom. He invites the Roman Christians to form a chorus to 'sing to the Father in Jesus Christ in honour of the fact that God has considered the Bishop of Syria worthy to be found being sent from the land of sunrise to the land of sunset. It is a good thing to set (like the sun) out of the world towards God, so that I may rise in him' (Rom. 2.2). This is at least a hint that Ignatius sees a connection between his being a bishop and his becoming a martyr, and, indeed, a highly significant martyr (as we have seen, he assures the Romans that they will never again have a chance to be associated with such an important event).

In the same passage in the letter to the Romans, Ignatius plays with the idea of silence. 'If you keep silent from me', he says (meaning that they are to leave him alone and not interfere to try to prevent his martyrdom), 'then I shall become a word of God; but if you are in love with my flesh, then I shall become a mere noise again' (Rom. 2.1).[28] At least in his own case, it seems that the silence of the bishop will be broken only in martyrdom, and only thanks to the silence of the Roman church. It is when he is, on the face of it, finally silenced in death that he will really become a word, instead of being just a noise; and he will become a word of God, like that word which came forth from the silence. The uniting of word and silence in his martyrdom is strikingly asserted.

As he does elsewhere, Ignatius goes on to talk about the importance of coherence between inner and outer, between what one is and what one professes to be, but he again adds a paradoxical twist to his message:

> Pray for power for me, within and without, so that I may not only talk, but be genuinely willing, not only be called a Christian, but actually be found to be one. For if I am found to be one, then I can both be called and be faithful, when I do not appear to the world. Nothing that appears is good. Our God, Jesus Christ, being in the Father, appears all the more. Christianity is not a matter of persuasive argument, but of greatness, when it is hated by the world. (Rom. 3.2–3)

Just as he believes that his word will become fully authentic only when he is martyred, Ignatius also believes that he himself will be fully visible as a believer only when he ceases to be visible to the world. His model, as always, is Christ, who appears all the more, now that he has disappeared from the world and is in the Father. The point is presumably similar to one that is made about God in the Hermetic writings: he appears more than anything else does, precisely because he does not appear. Anything that is visible in the ordinary way has a strictly limited visibility, but God, who is not visible as a distinct object on which our ordinary perception can alight, is visible everywhere in everything.[29] Similarly Jesus Christ, after his ascension, is no longer visible in the limited way in which his bodily presence was visible; but he is visible universally in his church. In the same manner Ignatius himself hopes that he will establish once and for all the integrity of inner and outer in his own case by successfully undergoing his martyrdom, the final proof of his genuineness as a Christian (he will be seen in what he does), even while it makes him invisible to the world.

In his letters Ignatius habitually speaks of himself in very derogatory terms. The least surprising thing is that he should consider himself to be 'at risk' (Eph. 12.1, Trall. 13.2). This seems natural enough, because he obviously might fail the final test of martyrdom. He is also aware that he might betray his discipleship of Jesus Christ right away by becoming conceited. People were evidently inclined to make much of him, as a confessor of the faith, apparently including people whom he regarded as insulting Christ by their erroneous beliefs (Trall. 4.1, Sm. 5.2); in response, he insists that his position as a prisoner for Christ ought to make him and does make him all the more afraid (Trall. 4.1, Phld. 5.1).

However, there seems to be more to his sentiments about himself than just a natural anxiety about the outcome of his journey towards martyrdom. He seems to have felt uneasy on his own account, as well as being unhappy about the state of his church, until he received his good news from Antioch. In his letter to Polycarp, after the good news has come, he says:

> For my own part, I am in better spirits, in a divine freedom from care, always provided that I attain to God by suffering, so that I will be found as your disciple in the resurrection. (Pol. 7.1)

Given his beliefs about the church, it would not be surprising if, finding himself effectively unchurched, he felt considerable qualms about his situation, even if he was sure that it was for the Lord that he was in chains. In his letters from Smyrna he several times contrasts his own position with that of other people, in terms most unflattering to himself.

> I know who I am and to whom I am writing. I am under condemnation, you have received mercy. I am at risk, you are established. (Eph. 12.1)

> Even if I am in bondage, by comparison with any one of you who have been set free, I am nothing. (Mag. 12.1)

> I am not so conceited as to give you orders as if I were an apostle. (Trall. 3.3)

> I do not give you orders, like Peter and Paul. They were apostles, but I am under condemnation; they were free, but I am still a slave. If I suffer, I shall become the freedman of Jesus Christ and arise free in him. For the moment I am learning in my bondage to covet nothing. (Rom. 4.3)

122

There is, of course, a perfectly obvious sense in which Ignatius was 'at risk' and 'under condemnation', even if it is unlikely that he was literally a slave (though even that has been suggested).[30] But this obvious sense seems to have no obvious application to the parties with whom Ignatius contrasts himself. The Ephesians have neither received any official pardon or acquittal from the Roman authorities, nor have they all successfully accomplished their martyrdom. The Magnesians have not been set free by the powers that are holding Ignatius captive. As for the apostles Peter and Paul, they had been as much condemned by the secular authorities as Ignatius, and it is hard to see what point there would be in contrasting their civil status with that of Ignatius.

It is only if we assume that Ignatius is referring to his status with regard to salvation, as well as to his legal and civil situation, that his comparisons make sense. The risk he faces is not simply that of failing to be a martyr, nor even that of failing to be a Christian by failing to be a martyr. He seems to see himself in danger of not really becoming a Christian in the first place; he feels himself to be bearing God's condemnation, to be still a slave to that condition of sin and death from which Christ came to redeem us. It is very striking how persistently he maintains that he is, as yet, barely even beginning to be a disciple. He tells the Ephesians that he is hoping to reach his goal of fighting the wild beasts in Rome, thanks to their prayers, 'so that by means of that attainment I may be able to be a disciple' (Eph. 1.2). Shortly afterwards he comments, 'I am not giving you orders, as if I were somebody. Even if I am in bondage in the Name, I am not yet brought to perfection in Jesus Christ. Now I possess a beginning of being a disciple' (Eph. 3.1). It is not martyrdom which puts him at risk; he is at risk anyway, and only the completion of his martyrdom will complete the process of his becoming a disciple. 'I shall truly be a disciple of Jesus Christ then', he writes to the Romans (4.2), 'when not even my body can be seen by the world.'

If we are right to believe that Ignatius had been denounced to the Roman authorities by disaffected members of his flock, then his comments become rather less puzzling. He had been condemned by the civil power, it is true, but at the same time he had effectively been condemned by his own church. Leaving Antioch in a state in which it was far from clear that he really had a church to belong to, he was denied the normal way of making visible his discipleship, so he had to refocus his hopes upon that last, most drastic way of expressing fidelity, martyrdom. Finding himself outside what I have called the 'chain of validation', in which life and reality are communicated from the Father to those who are in Christ, in the church, Ignatius now looks forward to his martyrdom as the occasion on which he will become a living and authentic human being. In deliberately paradoxical terms, he writes to the Romans about his hope to find life by dying:

> Excuse me, my brethren, do not get in the way of my living, do not want me to die. I want God, do not favour me with the world or deceive me with matter. Let me receive the pure light. When I get there, then I shall be human (*anthrōpos*). Let me be an imitator of the passion of my God. (Rom. 6.2–3)

Christ's passion is our resurrection (Sm. 5.3), and there is now no way open for Ignatius to share in that life-giving death, except by literally dying. That is how he will escape finally from the unreality which characterizes those who are outside the proper structures of the church.

Whether or not Ignatius had been a 'silent bishop' in Antioch, he was certainly a silenced bishop now. Since his message had, seemingly, failed in Antioch, he must hope for recognition now in the silence of what he does, becoming a word by giving his life for Christ. Having fallen victim to those who opposed him in his church, he interprets himself as being a sacrificial victim, offered for the church and its unity. 'I am your ransom (*antipsychon*)', he writes to the Ephesians and the Smyrnaeans (Eph. 21.1, Sm. 10.2); he says the same thing to Polycarp, subsequently adding the rider, 'I am a ransom for those who are subject to the bishop, the presbyters and the deacons' (Pol. 2.3, 6.1). In using the word *antipsychon* he implies that he is giving his life for theirs, he is dying so that they may live.

Elsewhere he also uses the word *peripsēma*, which literally means 'offscouring', but had come to be used fairly conventionally to mean little more than 'your faithful servant'. However, its original meaning could be reactivated even in connection with this weak, conventional use. Bishop Dionysius of Alexandria says that the word could be applied literally, not just conventionally, to those devoted Christians who sacrificed their own lives during the plague to look after the sick. Those who caught the plague and died, while the people they were looking after recovered and survived, were really taking on themselves the diseases of others.[31] There is also some evidence that the word was used in connection with the kind of sacrifice in which someone becomes a scapegoat, bearing the moral or ritual 'filth' of the people with him to destruction, so that the rest can live in peace and enjoy the favour of whatever god had been offended.[32] When Ignatius says that he is the '*peripsēma* of the cross' (Eph. 18.1), he may be using the word purely conventionally, but in Eph. 8.1 he combines it with explicitly sacrificial language, which suggests that he means it to be taken in a strong sense. 'I am your *peripsēma* and I consecrate myself for you Ephesians.' In this way he can make sacrificial sense of his own situation, in which he can hardly even recognize himself as a Christian. Bearing everything, as a bishop should, he has to bear even becoming 'scum', so that the churches may prosper, just as Christ became 'sin' for our sake, so that we might become 'the righteousness of God' (2 Cor 5:21).

Whatever doubts Ignatius may have had about his spiritual standing, those who read his letters will find it hard to doubt the intensity of his love for God and his utter fidelity to the gospel and to the church. Over and over again he expresses his yearning to 'attain to God' or 'to Jesus Christ' (Eph. 12.2, Mag. 14.1, Trall. 12.2, 13.3, Rom. 2.1, 4.1, 5.3, 9.2, Sm. 11.1, Pol. 7.1). What manner of man he was before his doom overtook him we have no way of knowing, but these extraordinary letters, wrung from him on his way to his death, reveal a hunger for God and a passionateness unlike anything that we find elsewhere in the writings of the Apostolic Fathers.

Ignatius tells the Ephesians that he hopes to write them a second, more systematic letter (Eph. 20.1). It would have been interesting to meet Ignatius in the guise of a systematic theologian. All the same, it is worth forgoing that pleasure for the fascinating gift he has left us. In the fiery outpourings of his ardent and uneasy soul, we can see traces of a more systematic understanding of the Christian faith, and in this chapter we have tried to interpret them more systematically than they appear in the letters. But it would be unfair to take our leave of him on this note. Above all else, he was a man in love, and it is as such that we should catch our last glimpse of him.

> While I am alive, I write to you, desiring to die. My desire is crucified[33] and there is in me no matter-loving fire, but a water which is living and speaking in me, saying within me, 'Come here to the Father'. I do not enjoy the food of corruption or the pleasures of this life. I want the bread of God, which is the flesh of Jesus Christ, born of the seed of David, and I want his blood to drink, which is imperishable charity. (Rom. 7.2)

Come fire and cross, come gangs of wild beasts, come knife and saw, come rack and mangling, let my whole body be pulped, let the worst punishments of the devil come upon me. All I ask is that I may attain to Jesus Christ. (Rom. 5.3)

Notes

1 In this chapter I am taking for granted the authenticity of the seven letters now generally admitted as genuine, in spite of the recent attempt by J. Ruis-Camps to stir up controversy afresh (*The Four Authentic Letters of Ignatius, the Martyr* [Rome, 1979]). The classic discussion of the evidence remains that of J. B. Lightfoot, *The Apostolic Fathers* (London, 1885), vol. II.1, pp. 70–414.

2 Polycarp, *Letter to the Philippians* 13.

3 Eusebius, *Hist. Eccl.* 3.36.

4 Eusebius, *Hist. Eccl.* 3.36; *Chronicle* (PL 27:607). On the dating, see Lightfoot, *op. cit.* II.2, pp. 435–72; P. N. Harrison, *Polycarp's Two Epistles to the Philippians* (Cambridge, 1936), pp. 209–30.

5 Eusebius, *Hist. Eccl.* 3.22, 3.36.

6 Cf. C. H. Kraeling, 'The Jewish community at Antioch', *Journal of Biblical Literature* 51 (1932), pp. 130–60; E. M. Smallwood, *The Jews under Roman Rule* (Leiden, 1981), pp. 358–9.

7 Cf. F. Watson, *Paul, Judaism and the Gentiles* (Cambridge, 1986), pp. 49–56.

8 Cf. R. M. Grant, 'Jewish Christianity at Antioch in the second century' in *Judéo-Christianisme: Recherches historiques et théologiques offertes en hommage au Cardinal Jean Daniélou* (Paris, 1972), pp. 97–108.

9 The Gnostics certainly ascribed a divine role to hypostatized Silence, beginning, it seems, with Simon Magus (Hippolytus, *Refutatio* 6.18.2; for a recent assessment of the authenticity of the *Apophasis Megalē* attributed to Simon, see Catherine Osborne, *Rethinking Early Greek Philosophy* [London, 1987], pp. 212–27). Silence also features in Valentinus's system: see Irenaeus, *Adv. Haer.* 1.1. However there is also evidence of an association between divinity and silence, or even of a divinization of Silence, in Hellenistic religion. Cf. Chaldaean Oracles, fragment 16 (ed. E. des Places [Paris, 1971]); Mesomedes, *Hymns* 1.1–3 (described as being 'Pythagorean') (ed. K. Horna [Vienna/ Leipzig, 1928]); K. Preisendanz (ed.), *Papyri Graecae Magicae* vol. I (Stuttgart, 1973), p. 92. Cf. also H. Schmidt, *Veteres Philosophi quomodo iudicaverint de Precibus* (Giessen, 1907), pp. 64–5. In the syncretistic world of late antiquity, it is usually fruitless to ask who is influencing whom; it is safest to say that it was just 'in the air' at the time to associate silence with divinity. Later philosophers took up the notion of divine silence, and it is most unlikely that they inherited it from the Gnostics. Cf. Proclus, *Commentary on the Timaeus*, ed. E. Diehl, vol. III (Leipzig, 1906), p. 222; *Chaldaean Extracts* 4, ed. Des Places, *ed. cit.*, p. 210. Also Damascius, *De Principiis*, ed. L. G.

Westerink (Paris, 1986), p. 84. For Proclus's locating of the highest God beyond silence, cf. *Commentary on the Parmenides* VII, ed. V. Cousin (Paris, 1864), col. 1171; Latin trans. by William of Moerbeke, ed. C. Steel, vol. II (Louvain, 1985), pp. 440, 505.

10 For the divinization of the One in Hellenistic Pythagoreanism, as the source of all things, cf. H. Thesleff, *The Pythagorean Texts of the Hellenistic Period* (Abo, 1965), pp. 59, 108.

11 Clement of Alexandria, *Protr.* 2.11.1, refers to the silencing of speaking wells and the general demise of prophetic waters; cf. also the alleged reply of Delphi to Julian the Apostate, that Apollo no longer has a 'speaking spring' (H. W. Parke and D. E. W. Wormell, *The Delphic Oracle* [Oxford, 1956], no. 476; J. Fontenrose doubts the authenticity of this response: *The Delphic Oracle* [Berkeley, 1978], p. 353).

12 Cf. especially H. Schlier, *Religionsgeschichtliche Untersuchungen zu den Ignatiusbriefen* (Giessen, 1929).

13 Justin Martyr, *I Apol.* 26.4; Irenaeus, *Adv. Haer.* I, 23.5.

14 Irenaeus I, 24.1–2. He is said to have been a contemporary of Basilides (Hippolytus, *Ref.* 7.28.1), who taught under Trajan's successor Hadrian (Clement of Alexandria, *Strom.* VII, 106.4), so may not already have been active in the reign of Trajan.

15 For the interpretation given here of the situation in Antioch and the circumstances of Ignatius's arrest, cf. Harrison, *op. cit.*, pp. 79–106; F. W. Schlatter, 'The restoration of peace in Ignatius' Antioch', *Journal of Theological Studies* NS 35 (1984), pp. 465–9.

16 Cf. in general O. Cullmann, 'Dissensions within the early church', *Union Seminary Quarterly Review* 22 (1967), pp. 83–92.

17 Pliny, *Letters* 96–97.

18 Eusebius, *Hist. Eccl.* 3.32.

19 It is impossible to make sense of Ignatius's use of the word *eucharistia* except on the assumption that it means 'the eucharist'; cf., for example, Phld. 4.1, Sm. 7.1.

20 It is a disputed question whether Ignatius accords any kind of primacy to the church of Rome, within the universal church. Cf. the sensible comments of P. T. Camelot on the opening of the Letter to the Romans in his Sources Chrétiennes edition (Paris, 1969), pp. 106–7.

21 It seems reasonable to interpret all the genitives in this clause in the same way, notwithstanding the curious reluctance of translators to do so. As I hope the ensuing exposition makes clear, there is good theological sense to be gleaned from them, if we do take them all in the same way.

22 For a slightly later testimony to the belief that people who were suffering for the faith were, so to speak, entitled to supernatural revelations, cf. *Passio Perpetuae* 4.

23 J. H. Srawley, *The Epistles of St Ignatius* (London, 1900), vol. I, p. 46.

24 Cf. P. Meinhold, *Studien zu Ignatius von Antiochien* (Wiesbaden, 1979), pp. 19–36; L. F. Pizzolato, 'Il silenzio del vescovo', *Aevum* 44 (1970), pp. 205–18.

25 Harrison, *op. cit.*, p. 97.

26 'The silence of bishops', *Harvard Theological Review* 43 (1950), pp. 169–72.

27 *Gospel of Peter* 10. There is an excellent edition of the text, with a substantial commentary, including discussions of date, place of origin and relationship to other early Christian writings, by M. G. Mara (Sources Chrétiennes vol. 201; Paris, 1973).

28 There is a textual problem here, but Lightfoot is surely right to prefer the reading implied by the ancient versions. The contrast between 'word' (*logos*) and 'noise' (*phōnē*) is not particularly recondite. In Irenaeus, *Adv. Haer.* I, 14.4 it is used to distinguish between merely hearing the sound (*phōnē*) of an utterance, and hearing it as a meaningful pronouncement (*logos*). In *Hermetica* 12.13 it is used to distinguish between animal noises and human speech.

29 *Hermetica* 5, entitled 'The unmanifest God is most manifest'. Cf. ibid., 11.22, on how God is manifested in everything.

30 Cf. Lightfoot's commentary on Rom. 4.3, *op. cit.*, II. 2, pp. 209–10.

31 Eusebius, *Hist. Eccl.* 7.22.

32 The fifth-century lexicographer Hesychius gives 'ransom' as one meaning of the word; the eighth-century scholar and Patriarch Photius tells us that it was applied to some unspecified annual sacrifice of a young man to Poseidon as an expiatory offering (*Lexicon*, ed. S. A. Naber [Leiden, 1865], p. 85).

33 Origen (prologue to the commentary on the Canticle, ed. W. A. Baehrens, p. 71) apparently took Ignatius's phrase, 'my *erōs* is crucified', to mean 'my Love (Christ) is crucified', and this has been echoed down the centuries and is still to be found in our hymnbooks: e.g. nos. 25, 26 and 27 in John and Charles Wesley's *Collection of Hymns*; F. W. Faber's well-known 'O come and mourn with me awhile'; G. R. Woodward's 'This joyful Eastertide'. Curiously, the oldest Christian hymnbook of all, the *Odes of Solomon*, contains the words 'My love is the Lord' (16.3). Nevertheless Greek usage and the context in Ignatius entirely rule out such an interpretation of his original sentence.

7

Polycarp

Polycarp is more interesting as a man and as a martyr than he is as a writer. At the time of his martyrdom, probably on 23 February 155,[1] he claimed to have been serving Christ for eighty-six years (*Mart.* 9.3), which means that, even if we assume that he was baptized as an infant, he must have been born no later than AD 69. His life did not merely reach back to apostolic times; he was himself personally acquainted with St John and 'others who had seen the Lord'.[2] Tertullian cites a tradition of the church of Smyrna to the effect that Polycarp was appointed its bishop by St John himself.[3] As we have seen, he was Bishop of Smyrna when Ignatius passed by on his way to his martyrdom.

Irenaeus treasured a vivid memory of having seen and heard Polycarp, when he was himself a child in Asia Minor, and he tells us how Polycarp talked about his own memories of the first generation of believers, who had 'seen the Lord'.[4] Because of his longevity, Polycarp served as a bridge between the apostolic age and the self-consciously Catholic orthodoxy of the latter part of the second century. By all accounts, it was a role he was ideally suited by his temperament to fill.

Not being and not desiring to be an original thinker himself, he was content to venerate the authority of the original apostles and of St Paul (cf. *Ep*. 3.1–2), and he seems to have had an almost naïve horror of heresy. One of his stories about St John portrays the apostle finding the early Gnostic heretic, Cerinthus, in the baths one day. Without lingering to take his own bath, John cried out, 'Let us flee, in case the baths collapse, since the enemy of truth, Cerinthus, is here!' On one occasion he himself met Marcion, who demanded to be recognized by him. 'I do recognize you,' he retorted, 'I recognize you as the first-born of Satan.'[5]

Very shortly before his martyrdom, the old man went to Rome to see Pope Anicetus in connection with the controversy about the date on which Easter should be celebrated; Polycarp's determination not to abandon the apostolic tradition he had received, combined with tact and good will on both sides, seems to have defused for the time being a disagreement which later flared up much more aggressively. While he was in Rome, Polycarp is said to have converted many of the followers of the heretics, Valentinus and Marcion, to the orthodox faith.[6] As a living witness to the original, apostolic tradition, he must have been a powerful argument in his own person against the pretended secret 'apostolic' traditions of the Gnostics.

What purports to be one letter of Polycarp survives, addressed to the Philippians. The first part of the text survives in Greek, but the rest is known only in a Latin version, except for one paragraph, which is quoted in Greek by Eusebius. Eusebius confirms that, at least by his day, the tradition ascribed to Polycarp only one letter.[7] Irenaeus, however, talks of 'letters' in the plural,[8] though he only specifically refers to one letter to the Philippians (clearly the one we possess).[9]

What makes it attractive to suspect that the surviving text is two letters or bits of two letters, rather than one, is that there appears to be a contradiction between the paragraph Eusebius quotes and a passage in the extant Greek portion of the rest of the text: Eusebius's paragraph and the sentence which follows it in the Latin translation imply that Ignatius has only recently left the region, and no definite news has yet been received about his martyrdom, whereas the other passage includes Ignatius among those who have already suffered with the Lord and are now with him 'in the place which is their due' (9.1–2). It is also remarkable how many of the New Testament writings are quoted or clearly alluded to in the main part of the letter, which, it has been argued, suggests a date much later than the letters of Ignatius. In 1936 P. N. Harrison ingeniously solved the problem by excising the paragraph cited by Eusebius and ascribing it to a separate letter.[10]

The separate letter thus created gives us a fascinating glimpse of what we may call the network of early Christian communications:

> You wrote to me, you and Ignatius, to ask that if anyone is
> going to Syria he would take your letters too. If I find a suit-

able opportunity, I will do it myself or by sending someone who can act on your behalf too. As you bid us, we are sending you the letters of Ignatius, those which he sent us and as many other letters as we have here. They are attached to this letter, and you will be able to benefit greatly from them. They contain faith and endurance and every kind of edification which pertains to our Lord. With regard to Ignatius himself and his companions, tell us anything you know for certain. (13.1-2)

It is interesting to learn that Ignatius's letters were in demand, even before definite news had been received of his martyrdom. Polycarp, devoted as he was to the apostolic tradition, was an ideal person to collect the letters of a faithful witness to that tradition, such as Ignatius.

Even if the text just quoted does not come from *the* letter to the Philippians, there is no reason to deny that it belongs to a letter sent to the same destination. We know from Ignatius's letter to Polycarp (8.1) that Ignatius was taken by his gaolers from Troas to Neapolis, which is not all that far from Philippi, so it is quite possible that the Philippian Christians were able to visit him and that he took the opportunity to write to Antioch. In his letter to Polycarp (7.2) he asks Polycarp to send a message there, presumably because he did not have time to write a letter himself—we have his word for it that he intended to write more letters from Troas, but was prevented by his sudden departure for Neapolis (Pol. 8.1). If we assume that Polycarp sent only a brief covering letter with his collection of Ignatius's letters, it is not improbable that the Philippian church preserved it by inserting it into his more extended epistle to them, so that the later tradition received them both as a single letter.

On the other hand, the arguments against the integrity of the single letter are not decisive. There was no particular reason to doubt that Ignatius was martyred, even if no news had yet been received, so, in a formal letter of exhortation Ignatius could be cited impressively and not implausibly as a martyr whom the Philippian church had actually seen on his way to martyrdom; this would not necessarily exclude the possibility of asking for news about him at the end of the letter, which was allowed by the genre to be more gossipy.

As for Polycarp's extensive use of the New Testament, this would be a much more powerful argument if we knew much more about the early diffusion of the New Testament writings. As it is, we should notice that Polycarp quite clearly does not know of any New

Testament 'scriptures'. He in fact disclaims any intimate knowledge of 'scripture':

> I am confident that you are well versed in the sacred writings, and nothing is hidden from you. Such a gift has not been granted to me. Only, as it says in these scriptures, 'Be angry and do not sin, and do not let the sun go down on your anger'. (12.1)

At first sight, this is a quotation from Ephesians 4:26 as 'scripture', but it is most unlikely that this is what Polycarp means. His letter shows that he is deeply familiar with the New Testament writings; what is strikingly absent is evidence of any real acquaintance with the Old Testament. What we should infer from the passage just quoted is that Polycarp is still using the term 'sacred writings' (scripture) to mean only the Old Testament, which he admits he does not know well. The 'scripture' he intends to cite is Psalm 4:4 ('Be angry and do not sin'), but he illustrates his ignorance of the Old Testament, intentionally or unintentionally, by citing it via St Paul.

Polycarp in fact represents a relatively new kind of Christian. Not having any Jewish background, he has apparently never succeeded in immersing himself in the traditional scriptures; instead he has immersed himself in the apostolic tradition, and it is quite in line with all that we know of him that he should have been an avid collector of the apostolic writings which later formed the New Testament scriptures. And he is already effectively treating them as scripture. His language is permeated by 'New Testament' allusions, just as that of Barnabas is impregnated with the Old Testament. Just as the older Christianity, close to its roots in Judaism, developed its theological language by weaving together morsels from all over the Old Testament, Polycarp has developed, if not a theological language, at least a language of edification, by weaving together phrases that he has culled from a surprisingly wide range of 'apostolic' writings. This is indeed one of the most remarkable features of his letter (and it makes no difference whether we are dealing with a single letter or with two). He has clearly absorbed at least the Gospel of Matthew, almost all the Pauline epistles, including the Pastoral Epistles, the Acts of the Apostles, 1 Peter and 1 John. As a sample of how he weaves his own message out of his apostolic sources, it is worth looking at a passage near the beginning of the letter (which can also serve to give us a taste of his worthy, but somewhat banal, message).

I rejoiced greatly in our Lord Jesus Christ . . . that the firm
root of your faith, proclaimed from ancient times, has
remained to this day and is still bearing fruit in our Lord Jesus
Christ, who endured even to face death for our sins, whom
God raised up, having loosened the pangs of Hades (Acts
2:24); not having seen him, you believe in him with unutterable
and glorified joy (1 Pet 1:8), a joy to which many desire to
come, knowing that you have been saved by grace, not by
works (Eph 2:8–9), but by the will of God through Jesus Christ
(cf. 1 Thess 5:18). Therefore gird up your loins (1 Pet 1:13) and
serve God in fear (Psalm 2:11) and truth, abandoning the
empty verbiage and deception of the populace and believing in
him who raised our Lord Jesus Christ from the dead and gave
him glory (1 Pet 1:21) and a throne at his right side, to whom
everything is subject, in heaven and on earth (cf. Eph 1:22,
Phil 2:10), whom everything that breathes serves, who is
coming as judge of the living and the dead (Acts 10:42), whose
blood God will require of those who do not obey him. And he
who raised him from the dead will raise us too (2 Cor 4:14), if
we do his will and walk in his commandments (cf. 2 John 6)
and love what he has loved, abstaining from all unrighteousness, covetousness, love of money, backbiting, false witness,
not returning evil for evil or abuse for abuse (1 Pet 3:9) or
blow for blow or curse for curse, remembering what the Lord
said in his teaching: Do not judge, so that you will not be
judged; forgive and you will be forgiven; have mercy, so that
you may receive mercy; the measure you give will be the measure you get in return. And: Blessed are the poor and those
who are persecuted for righteousness' sake, for theirs is the
kingdom of God (cf. Matt 7:1, 6:14, 5:7, 7:2, 5:3, 5:10). (1.1 –
2.3)

Apart from general exhortations in this vein, Polycarp has specific
words of fairly commonplace moral advice for specific groups of
people: wives, widows, deacons, young people and presbyters all
receive their own little message.

One point which is worth noting is Polycarp's instructions on how
the Philippians ought to react to a priest called Valens and his wife,
who have evidently disgraced themselves in some way unbecoming
to the priestly office:

I am very distressed, brethren, for him and for his wife; may
the Lord grant them true repentance. And you too must be

sober in this matter. Do not think of such people as enemies, but call them back as fallible and erring members of your body, so that you may save the whole of your body. If you do this, you build yourselves up too. (11.4)

Apart from the moral exhortations, there is little of any doctrinal interest. Polycarp does include a short credal section in his letter, but it is undeveloped speculatively:

Anyone who does not confess that Jesus Christ has come in flesh is an antichrist, and whoever does not acknowledge the martyrdom [or witness] of the cross is of the devil, and whoever manipulates the words of the Lord to suit his own desires and says that there is no resurrection and no judgment is a first-born of Satan. So let us abandon the fatuity and the false doctrines of the populace and return to the traditional word handed down to us from the beginning. (7.1-2)

Soon after Polycarp's martyrdom, the whole story of the persecution and of Polycarp's own initial flight and subsequent betrayal, arrest, trial and execution, was written up by the local church and circulated throughout the region. It is of considerable historical, but little speculative, interest. It is explicitly concerned to show that Polycarp's was a 'martyrdom according to the gospel' (*Mart.* 1.1), unlike the débâcle of a would-be martyr who handed himself over to the authorities of his own accord, but then lost his nerve and apostatized. His sad story receives the tart comment, 'So we do not approve of people who present themselves [sc. for martyrdom], because this is not the teaching of the gospel' (*Mart.* 4).

One small point of interest is that the account of the martyrdom not merely uses the phrase 'the catholic church' to apply to the universal church (*Mart.* tit.), as Ignatius does, but also refers to 'the catholic church in Smyrna' (16.2), evidently using 'catholic' in a doctrinal, not a geographical, sense, to distinguish the 'catholic church' from the heretics.

Notes

1   The classic discussion of the date is that of Lightfoot, *The Apostolic Fathers* (London, 1885), II.1, pp. 629-702. Cf. also T. D. Barnes, 'A note on Polycarp', *Journal of Theological Studies* NS 18 (1967), pp. 433-7; P. T. Camelot, in the 4th edition of his Sources Chrétiennes volume of Ignatius and Polycarp (Paris, 1969), pp. 199-200. The date

155 is based on the evidence of what is probably an appendix to the account of Polycarp's martyrdom (*Mart.* 21), which says that he was martyred on Saturday, 23 February. 23 February was a Saturday in 155, and this is a plausible date for the proconsulship of Quadratus, which is used to date the year of the martyrdom in *Mart.* 21. No other date fits the evidence so completely. Eusebius has a quite different date, and recently P. Brind'Amour has argued in favour of 167 on the basis of Eusebius ('La date du martyre de Saint Polycarpe', *Analecta Bollandiana* 98 (1980), pp. 456–62), and F. Halkin has given his support to this (ibid. 101 [1983], p. 226); however Brind'Amour has to resort to evidence from a much later period to show that 'great Sabbath' can mean Sunday in Christian Greek, to accommodate the fact that in 167, 23 February fell on a Sunday. And the argument is pointless anyway, as the text of *Mart.* 7–8 shows quite clearly that Saturday, not Sunday, is meant. Since Eusebius's notice, at this point, is manifestly inaccurate (he puts together the martyrdoms of Polycarp and Pionius, but Pionius was martyred under Decius in the middle of the third century) (Eusebius, *Chronicle*, PL 27:627; the real date of Pionius's martyrdom is given in the Acta of his martyrdom), it seems safe to ignore him here, and follow the cue given by the *Martyrium Polycarpi*.

2 Eusebius, *Hist. Eccl.* 5.20.
3 Tertullian, *De Praescriptione Haereticorum* 32.2.
4 Irenaeus, *Adv. Haer.* III, 3.4.
5 Ibid.
6 Ibid.
7 Eusebius, *Hist. Eccl.* 3.36, 4.14.
8 In Eusebius 5.20.
9 *Adv. Haer., loc. cit.*
10 *Polycarp's Two Epistles to the Philippians* (Cambridge, 1936).

8

The 'Second Letter of Clement'

The little document presented in the manuscripts as 'the second letter of Clement to the Corinthians' is, as is now generally recognized, not a letter at all; and, since its style and its use of Greek are quite different from anything we find in the 'first' letter of Clement to the Corinthians, it is difficult to believe that the Clement who wrote the letter is also the author of the 'second letter'. The renown of Clement was such that a variety of other people's works came to shelter under the patronage of his name, and *2 Clement* can safely be numbered among them.

The modern practice of calling it a 'homily' is, however, not entirely accurate either. The text makes it clear that a congregation is being addressed in a liturgical context (17.3), but it is explicitly being *read* to the people, apparently by the person who has just been doing the scriptural readings (19.1). His appeal is distinguished from the exhortations given by the presbyters, in a way which strongly suggests that its author is not himself a presbyter (17.3). Is he perhaps an official reader (lector)? The rank of reader is attested quite early on,[1] and may well have existed almost from the beginning; there is some evidence for the existence of readers among the officials of the synagogue in some places.[2] But the office of reader is nowhere associated with any right to preach in the church. Yet we cannot suppose that the 'reader' of *2 Clement* is merely reading out someone else's homily, as his use of the first person singular shows the author and the reader to be identical. The speaker who identifies himself in 15.1 as giving the congregation counsel, and as hoping to gain salvation for himself thereby, must be the author; but it is

136

almost impossible to imagine that he is not the same 'I' as the one who refers to himself in 19.1 as reading the appeal and hoping for salvation from its good effects, and who goes on, 'The reward I am asking from you is whole-hearted repentance'.

The only parallel I can suggest is the message Hermas presents himself as having received by divine revelation, which he is charged to *read* to the congregation in Rome (Hermas, Vis. 2.4, 8.3), and indeed to read repeatedly (Vis. 5, 25.5–7). Hermas too nowhere presents himself as being a presbyter, and he speaks of presbyters as if they are a class to which he does not belong (Vis. 2.4, 8.2–3). Conceivably the 'preacher' of *2 Clement* was in a similar position.

Various conjectures have been made about the date and location of the homily, but it is impossible to arrive at any confident conclusions, though a date in the first half of the second century seems likely.[3]

The preacher situates himself and his hearers unambiguously in the context of the church of the Gentiles. Previously they had worshipped idols, mere human products, and their life was no better than death; they were lost in error, with no hope of salvation (1.6–7). Now, thanks to the mercy of Christ, 'we are alive and do not sacrifice to dead gods or worship them, but, through him, we know the Father of truth' (3.1).

With perhaps a certain complacency the author cites Isaiah 54:1, 'Rejoice, you barren women who do not give birth . . . the children of the desolate woman are more than those of the woman with a husband'. 'Our church', he interprets this as meaning (the church of the Gentiles, that is) 'was barren before children were given to her . . . Our people seemed to be desolate, without God, but now we are believers we have become more numerous than those who seemed to have God. And another scripture says, "I have not come to call righteous people, but sinners". He says this, because it is those who are perishing who must be saved. That is the great and wonderful thing: not securing things that were already standing, but making firm what was falling. So Christ wanted to save what was perishing, and he saved many, coming and calling us who were already perishing' (2.1–7).

What the preacher is afraid of, though, is that his congregation does not appreciate the seriousness of their own conversion, and in particular its moral consequences. He begins his address with a call to recognize Christ as God and as 'judge of the living and the dead'. 'And', he goes on, 'we must not take a small view of our salvation. If we take a small view of him, there is little that we hope to receive from him.' Misjudging the seriousness of the gospel leads to sin, 'and we sin, not realizing the situation from which we were called, by whom we were called, or to what place we were called, or how much Jesus Christ endured to suffer for our sake' (1.1–3).

Maybe the preacher was exaggerating, as preachers do, but he gives us a lurid picture of a church full of people who reckoned that their change of religion was quite compatible with continuing to live by worldly standards of morality. Even the pagans were shocked.

> The Lord says, 'My name is blasphemed everywhere among the nations', and, 'Woe to the person through whom my name is blasphemed'. And how is it blasphemed? In your not doing what I want. The nations hear the words of God from our mouths and are amazed at their goodness and greatness. Then they learn what we do and how unworthy it is of the words we speak, and they turn to insult, saying that it is all a story and a deception. When they hear from us that God says, 'It is no thanks to you if you love those who love you; what does deserve credit is if you love your enemies and those who hate you', when they hear this, they are amazed at its extraordinary generosity. But when they see that, not only do we not love those who hate us, we do not even love those who love us, they laugh at us and God's name is brought into disrepute. (13.2–4)

'Let us repent now, brethren,' is our preacher's general comment, 'let us be vigilant with regard to good. For we are full of much folly and wickedness' (13.1).

One reason why people do not 'serve God with a pure heart' is that they do not believe his promise (11.1). This picks up the author's initial complaint that we do not appreciate 'the place to which we have been called' (1.2). In response, the preacher cites the same apocryphal prophecy as Clement:

> The undecided are wretched, who doubt in their hearts and say, 'We heard all this long ago, even in the time of our fathers. We have waited for it day after day and not seen any of it fulfilled.' Fools, compare yourselves to a tree. Take the vine: first it produces leaves, then comes the branch, then the unripe grape, and then the ripe fruit. (11.2–3)

So we must wait in hope. God, who promised, is faithful, so 'if we perform righteousness before God, we shall come into his kingdom and receive the promised blessings, which no ear has heard nor eye seen, nor has it entered the heart of anyone' (11.6–7).

The call *into* the kingdom is at the same time a call *out of* the ways of this world. We must regard the things of this world as 'foreign'; by desiring them, we fall from the righteous way (5.6). 'The Lord says, "No servant can be a slave to two masters". . . . This world and the world to come are two enemies. This world proclaims adultery, corruption, love of money, deceit, but the other world renounces these things. So we cannot be friends of both of them' (6.1–5).

The choice between the two 'worlds' is made all the more urgent by the risk of persecution. This world puts pressure on Christians in two ways. Even without persecution, it constantly calls us to abide by its values, which is why we must not seek to 'please men' (13.2). But it also faces us with threats, which is why we must fear God and not fear men (4.4). The world offers us the reward of present enjoyment, but such enjoyment is shortlived (6.6) and leads to torment (10.4). Worldly pleasures, like 'adultery, malicious gossip and rivalry' (4.3), are not in accordance with God's commandments. Our preacher cites a saying of the Lord apparently responding directly to the fact that 'we[4] are doing these things' (perhaps a prophetic utterance delivered in the community): 'If you are with me, gathered together in my lap, and do not do what I command, I will cast you out and say to you, "Depart from me, I do not know where you have come from, you workers of lawlessness" ' (4.5). If we disobey his commandments, 'nothing will rescue us from eternal punishment' (6.7).

Conversely, fidelity to the will of Christ will win us the 'great and wonderful promise of Christ and the repose of the kingdom to come and of eternal life' (5.5, 6.7). Only those who are ignorant of the 'luxuriousness' of the blessings which are promised would choose the passing delights of the present world (10.4). The boons of the world to come are 'imperishable benefits' (6.6).

Accordingly we must not be afraid to leave this world (which is only a temporary abode anyway).

> The Lord said, 'You will be like lambs in the midst of wolves'. Peter answered, 'Then what if the wolves rend the lambs?' Jesus said to Peter, 'Once they are dead, lambs should not fear wolves. And you too should not fear those who kill you and can then do nothing to you; you should fear him who has power over soul and body after you are dead, to cast you into the Gehenna of fire.' (5.1–4)

It does not sound, from what our preacher says, as if his church is actually being persecuted at the moment, but persecution is a real possibility, and it brings into sharp focus the obligation on Christians to confess Christ. Through him we have received knowledge of 'the Father of truth'. 'And what is knowledge in his regard? What else, but not to deny the one through whom we know him' (3.1). If we confess him before men, he will confess us before his Father. And what does it mean to confess our saviour? It means 'doing what he says and not disobeying his commandments' (3.2–4). It is not enough to call him 'Lord'. 'Let us confess him in our deeds, in loving one another, in not committing adultery or speaking ill of each other or behaving as each other's rivals. We ought to be sympathetic to one another, and not be lovers of money' (4.3).

We owe Christ a return for all that he has given us (1.3). We have been 'sealed' as his in baptism, so we should 'keep our baptism holy and undefiled'. If we do not, what confidence can we have when our time comes to enter God's kingdom? If we are not discovered to 'have holy, righteous works', who will be our advocate then? (6.9). For those who have not 'kept the seal', 'their worm will not die and their fire will not be extinguished and they will be a spectacle for all flesh' (7.6).

We have a contest on our hands. In a worldly contest it is only those who struggle hard and compete properly who win a crown. Anyone who is caught cheating is punished and expelled from the arena. So we must not try to cheat in the contest for immortality. 'Let us struggle so that we shall all be crowned . . . and if we cannot all be crowned, at least let us come close to a crown' (7.1–5).

It is tempting to interpret the 'crown' here as meaning the crown of martyrdom, as in Hermas (Sim. 8.3, 69.6), in which case there is nothing problematic about hoping that we shall at least come close to a crown. If the contest is, more generally, the struggle to live a decent Christian life, it is less clear what benefit there would be in nearly, but not quite, winning the struggle. However, a confession made by the preacher later on must give us pause.

> I myself am utterly sinful, I have not yet escaped temptation, but even though I am still in the middle of the devil's instruments, I strive to pursue righteousness, so that I may prevail at least to the extent of coming close to it, fearing the impending judgement as I do. (18)

In the light of this confession, we should probably interpret our author as meaning that the Christian life as such, even without persecution, is a contest, in which the important thing is that we should struggle to win it, even if we do not quite succeed. So the crown it is worth even getting close to is probably the reward of a successful Christian life as such (as it is must be in 20.2), without any thought of martyrdom. The author of *2 Clement* evidently agrees with the Didachist, that it is worth doing what we can, even if we do fall short of perfect obedience to God's law.

If this is what our preacher means, it is probably significant that he constantly stresses the need for wholeheartedness. We must honour Christ, not just with our lips, but 'with all our heart and with all our mind' (3.4). We must repent of our sins 'with all our heart' (8.2). We must entrust ourselves to the God who heals us, and the price he demands is that we repent 'with a sincere heart' (9.8). Instead of being undecided and doubtful, we must serve God 'with a pure heart' (11.1-2). At the judgement the righteous will glorify God, saying that the hope of those who served God whole-heartedly will be realized (17.7).

The moral is surely that, even if our practice leaves something to be desired, at least we must be totally sincere and unhesitating in our allegiance to Christ. We must certainly aim to do what he commands, but the opposite of doing this is, in the language of our author, not 'going against' (*parabainō*) the commandments, but 'failing to hear them properly' (*parakouō*) (3.4, 6.7, 15.5).[5] In another suggestive phrase, the author refers to 'those among us who were irreverent and who treated the commandments of Jesus Christ dishonestly' (17.6).

At the judgement, the crucial consideration will be whether or not we have been faithful to Christ. It is true that, at the time of his 'manifestation', he will rescue us 'in accordance with what each one of us has done' (17.4), but the people who will be condemned to the punishment of 'unquenchable fire' are those who 'turned aside and denied Jesus in their words or in their deeds' (17.7). 'Unbelievers' (and this evidently means supposedly Christian unbelievers) 'will see his glory and might and they will be astounded to see that Jesus is king of the world. They will say, "Woe to us that it is you, and we did not realize it, we did not believe, we were not docile to the presbyters who told us about our salvation" ' (17.5).

This brings us back to where our preacher started: we must be serious about our salvation, and not decorate an essentially unconverted attitude with an appearance of religion. If we take it seriously, then our Christian life contains ways of dealing with stray sins.

> Let us repent whole-heartedly. . . . Let us collaborate with each other to lead even the weak towards the good, so that we may

all be saved, and let us convert and admonish each other. Let us not only give the appearance of believing now [i.e. while we are in church] and paying attention when we are admonished by the presbyters, but when we return home too let us remember the Lord's commandments and not be dragged off instead by worldly desires. Rather let us meet together more frequently and try to make progress in the Lord's precepts, so that all of us, with a common mind, may be gathered together into life. (17.2–3)

Let us not take it badly and become indignant in our foolishness, when anyone admonishes us and tries to convert us from unrighteousness to righteousness. Sometimes we do not realize it, when we do evil, because of the indecisiveness and lack of faith that there is in our hearts. (19.2)

The primary way in which we show our fidelity to Christ and our dissociation of ourselves from worldly values is by loving one another (4.3), and 'love covers a multitude of sins' (16.4). So, if we do sin, an excellent way of doing penance is to give alms. 'Fasting is better than prayer, but almsgiving is better than both of them. . . . Prayer made with a good conscience rescues us from death. . . . Almsgiving alleviates the burden of sin' (16.4).[6]

Our author, like Barnabas, seems to see a particular application to preachers like himself of the principle that acts of love outweigh sins. 'So, brothers and sisters, after the God of truth [i.e. after the Scripture readings] I am reading you an appeal to pay attention to the Scriptures, so that you will save both yourselves and the reader in your midst' (19.1). 'I think that it is no small counsel that I have given you about self-control. If anyone acts on it, he will not regret it, but will save himself and me, who gave him this counsel. There is no small reward in turning towards salvation a soul which has gone astray and is perishing' (15.1).

The return that we can make to the God who created us is that both speaker and audience should speak and hear with faith and love. If we abide by our faith, then we can pray confidently to the God who says, 'While he is still speaking, I shall say, "Look, I am here!" ' . . . The Lord is telling us that he is more ready to give than we are to ask' (15.2–4).

While we have time, then, let us turn to the God who called us, while he is still ready to receive us. . . . If we overcome our own soul by not carrying out its wicked desires, then we shall share in the mercy of Jesus. But you must know that the day of judgement is coming like a burning oven. (16.1–3)

During this life, there seems to be no limit to the possibility of repentance and conversion. But the time limit is rigorous:

While we are on earth, let us repent. We are clay in the hand of the craftsman. If a potter is making a pot and it goes wrong or breaks in his hands, then he refashions it again. But once he has reached the point of putting it in the fiery oven, there is nothing more he will be able to do for it. In the same way it is while we are in this world in the flesh that we must repent wholeheartedly of the evil things we have done, so that we may be saved by the Lord, while we have time for repentance. After we have gone out of the world, we can no longer confess or repent there. (8.1–3)

Our author clearly takes a gloomy view of his own and his congregation's moral performance. But, he says, if that were all, it would be tolerable. What aggravates the situation intolerably is that there are people persistently putting forward a wrong teaching, to the effect that this flesh is not judged or resurrected, and that souls are blameless. They are unaware that they and their hearers will have to face a double judgement (of body and soul, that is) (9.1, 10.5).

These heterodox teachers are presumably to be identified with the people who 'adduce human fears, choosing present enjoyment rather than the promise which is to come' (10.3). Their denial of the resurrection and judgement of the flesh enables them to rid the gospel of all its awkwardnesses. If the soul can remain guiltless, whatever we do in the flesh, then there is no need to practise difficult virtues like chastity and control of our gossiping tongues, nor, should there be a threat of persecution, will there be any need to risk our lives by insisting on making any outward confession of Christ. A purely interior version of Christianity need pose no challenge to anyone's timidity or self-indulgence.

Similarly comfortable claims recur in certain forms of Gnosticism, but there is no sign in our text of any of the distinctive tenets of Gnosticism or of the typically Gnostic sophisms used to justify evading the challenge of martyrdom. Even apart from Gnosticism, we have found in Hermas and Ignatius signs that there were people exploiting a radical dissociation of flesh and spirit in order to play down the significance of the flesh, with lamentable consequences both for morality and for honesty in the face of persecution.

The most likely background to the heretics in question in *2 Clement* is, I suspect, the pagan mystery religions. It is clear that the church addressed by the preacher is one in which Christians are living in the midst of unconverted pagans (hence the 'commandment' which the church has, bidding her draw people away from idols: 17.1). And it looks as if at least some of the Christians, once they go home from church, are easily drawn back into the attitudes of the world around them (which is why the preacher calls for them to come together more often precisely as Christians: 17.3). They do not really believe that Jesus is the judge of the living and the dead (1.1) or the king of the world (17.5). For them, probably, Christianity was no more than a kind of insurance policy for the hereafter, enabling them to live comfortable, worldly lives here and now, confident that after death their souls would be admitted to some sort of Elysian paradise, with no significant moral qualifications required.

In response, our preacher stresses that it is while we are in the flesh that we must make our confession of Christ, and that this confession has serious moral implications (8.2–3, 3.4). And the flesh is all-important in the whole process of our salvation. The soul, far from being guiltless, is the source of our temptations and must accordingly be 'overcome' (16.2, 17.7).

Our author develops his theory of the flesh in two stages: first, with reference to Christ, and then with reference to the church.

The complaint about the false doctrine that the flesh is neither judged nor raised comes after the preacher's insistence that it is on this earth, in this flesh, that we must repent and make our confession of faith. It is 'by keeping the flesh pure and by observing the commandments of the Lord that we shall receive eternal life'. The Lord is quoted as saying, 'If you have not kept the little thing, who will give you the big thing?' and this is interpreted as meaning that we are to 'keep the flesh pure and the [baptismal] seal unspotted, in order to receive eternal life' (8.4–6). Then comes the first mention of the heretical doctrine, in response to which the preacher reminds us that it was 'in this flesh' that we were saved and 'saw the light', and therefore we must guard our flesh 'as God's temple'. We were called in the flesh, and it is in the flesh that we 'shall come' (i.e. return at the resurrection). Christ the Lord, who saved us, 'was first of all spirit, but he became flesh and that is how he called us. Similarly we too will receive our reward in this flesh' (9.1–5). Although the point is not developed, the author's implicit argument must be that the incarnation is the key to our understanding of salvation: if the beginning of our salvation was the coming of Christ in the flesh to us who are in the flesh, then the end of our salvation must also be in the flesh. And the linking together of the need to keep our flesh pure and the need to keep the baptismal seal unspotted implies that we are meant to recall that it was our flesh that was sealed in baptism.

In spite of our author's belief that adultery is one of the most pronounced features of worldly life, which Christians must therefore specially renounce (4.3, 6.4), it is quite clear that he is not particularly thinking of sexual morality, when he talks about keeping the flesh pure. At the end of his little demonstration of the importance of the flesh and the need to keep it pure, he concludes, 'Let us therefore love one another, so that we may all come to the kingdom of God' (9.6). In early Christian writings, 'love' is habitually a practical virtue, meaning actual kindness to and service of other people, with little or no reference to interior sentiment or emotion. This is why Clement, in his letter to the Corinthians, formulates the obvious objection to the doctrine of justification by faith with the question, 'What are we to do, then, brethren? Shall we refrain from good works and abandon charity?' (1 Clem. 33.1). Similarly Ignatius complains that heretics who deny the flesh of Christ 'have no concern for charity', clearly meaning practical charity towards those in need (Sm. 2, 6.2). Charity sums up the whole 'outwardness' of Christian morality, which stands or falls with people's beliefs about the seriousness of the flesh.

Practical charity and mutual help are obviously important aspects of what it means to belong to the church (cf. 4.3, 17.2); but our preacher has a view of the church which gives it a much greater significance than we might expect. If we do the will of God, 'we shall belong to the first church, the spiritual church, which was created before the sun and the moon' (14.1). This is recognizably the church, as we met her in Hermas, the first-born of all creation. But the 'living church' is also the body of Christ, and our author applies to Christ and his church what is said in Genesis about the first human beings: 'God made mankind male and female' (Gen 1:27). 'The male is Christ, the female is the church.' And 'the Bible and the apostles' are cited as saying that the church has not just now come into existence; it is from above.

For it was spiritual, like our Jesus, but was revealed in the last days to save us. The church, being spiritual, was manifested in the flesh of Christ, showing us that, if anyone keeps her in the flesh and does not corrupt her, he will receive her in the Holy Spirit. The flesh is the antitype of the Spirit. So no one who corrupts the antitype will receive the real thing.

What this means, as our preacher explains, is:

Keep the flesh, so that you will receive the Spirit. If we say that the flesh is the church and the Spirit is Christ, then anyone who insults the flesh insults the church. And no one like that will share in the Spirit, which is Christ. Such is the life and incorruptibility that this flesh can receive, when the Holy Spirit cleaves to it, and no one can either explain or state what God has prepared for his chosen ones. (14.2–5)

As an argument, the author's plea is hardly cogent or even honest, but he evokes a pattern of associations which is genuinely appealing. The 'incarnation' of the church underlines the significance of the flesh as such, and of our 'fleshly' belonging to the church. Respect for the 'flesh' of the church means both respecting the flesh of Christ, in which the church became 'incarnate', and respecting in our outward behaviour the integrity of the human person and of the human society which we ordinarily call the church. It is by our belonging to the church in the flesh in an authentic way that we shall come to belong to the spiritual church, which was created before the sun and the moon. And no one can say what an immensity of blessing that will mean.

The insistence on the flesh does not mean that a merely outward religion is, after all, sufficient. Our author has warned us often enough of the importance of sincerity and whole-heartedness. What matters is the harmony and unity of flesh and soul, of inner and outer, and this is affirmed in an apocryphal text we have already encountered, which our author duly cites. After exhorting us not to become doubtful because of the apparent delay in the fulfilment of God's promises, he tells us that, when the Lord was asked when his kingdom would come, he replied, 'When the two become one, and the outer as the inner, and the male with the female, neither male nor female'.[7] The 'two becoming one' our preacher interprets as referring to what happens when we speak the truth to each other: there is one soul, without hypocrisy, in two bodies. 'The outer as the inner' refers to the body ('the outer') and the soul ('the inner'); the soul must be manifest in good works, just as the body is manifest. And 'the male with the female, neither male nor female' means that a brother looks at a sister without 'thinking anything feminine about her, nor does she think anything masculine about him' (12.3–5). This last comment must be taken as alluding to the overcoming of the embarrassment attendant upon sexuality, which the apocryphal text cited by our author almost certainly mentioned.[8] How far our author was aware of or interested in the more daring speculation that this topic engendered in some circles and the more adventurous practices that sometimes went with it, we cannot tell.[9] He seems content with a fairly humdrum interpretation of the restoration of unity which is the antidote, brought by Christ, to the multiple fragmentation from which fallen humanity suffers.

'When you do these things, he says, the kingdom of my Father will come' (12.6). Our preacher evidently does not want to claim that 'these things' are already to be found in the Christian church. 'Paradise restored' is, for him, still something to be hoped for, not something to be acted out in the church.

However, it is not only due to our failure to live up to redemption that the coming of the kingdom is delayed. This life is a kind of athletic trial, for which we hope to be crowned in the future. And 'none of the righteous obtained quick results'. 'If God gave the just their reward in a hurry, then at once we would be practising trade, not religion, and it would appear that we were being righteous in pursuit of profit, not piety' (20.2–4). The delay in the coming of the kingdom gives us a chance to show that we are genuinely motivated by reverence for God and not just out for a quick supernatural buck.

Notes

1   Hippolytus, *Apostolic Tradition* 11; Didascalia, trans. R. H. Connolly (Oxford, 1929), p. 90.
2   Cf. S. Safrai and M. Stein (eds), *The Jewish People in the First Century*, vol. I (Assen, 1974), p. 498.
3   Militating against too early a date is the fact that the New Testament is cited as 'scripture' (2.4); but the lack of any reference to Gnosticism in a document so concerned about false doctrine suggest that *2 Clement* cannot be dated too far into the second century.
4   This seems the more plausible reading; the manuscripts are divided between 'we' and 'you'.
5   Cf. Hermas, Vis. 4.2, 23.6, where Hermas plays on 'hearing' (*akouō*) and 'mishearing' (*parakouō*), the latter being connected with indecisiveness (*dipsychia*). *2 Clement* never uses the more common word, *parabainō* (transgress).
6   This list of fasting, prayer and almsgiving, as the three essential ways of expiating one's sins, which became classic and was taken for granted in

the Middle Ages (cf. Augustine, *Sermons* 9.11.17, PL 38:88; Leo the Great, *Sermons* 12.4, PL 54:171C; William of Auxerre, *Summa Aurea* IV 11.2, ed. J. Ribaillier [Grottaferrata, 1985], p. 272; Raymund of Penyafort, *Summa de Poenitentia* III [Rome, 1603], pp. 467–8), seems already to have been conventional: cf. Matthew 6; Gospel of Thomas, logion 14 (logion 104 makes it clear that these works are intended as remedies for sin).

7   Cf. above, Chapter 4, note 1.

8   In Clement of Alexandria, *Strom.* III 92.2, the text runs, 'When you trample the garment of shame, and when the two become one, and the male with the female, neither male nor female'. Logion 22 and 37 in the Gospel of Thomas seem to be an amplification of the same text; the latter in particular makes it clear that a return to the unembarrassed nakedness of prelapsarian paradise is envisaged. Cf. Irenaeus, *Demonstration* 14, on the innocent sexuality of Adam and Eve before the Fall; for a later application of the same idea to the stripping off of one's clothes at baptism, cf. Cyril of Jerusalem, *Mystagogical Catecheses* 2.2; for a moral, ascetic application, cf. *Liber Graduum* 15.3.

9   In the Gospel of Thomas, anyway, the overcoming of sexual differentiation is seen as a return to the aboriginal condition of Adam, before the creation of Eve, when he was effectively androgynous (cf. G. Quispel, *Makarius, das Thomasevangelium und das Lied von der Perle* [Leiden, 1967], p. 32; J. E. Ménard, *L'Évangile selon Thomas* [Leiden, 1975], pp. 113–15). The practice of chaste cohabitation (cf. above, p. 87) is probably intended as a practical demonstration of the return to prelapsarian sexual innocence.